Forward

There are great difficulties in writing true crime stories especially about murder and rapes as there is an importance on keeping them as accurate to the truth as possible yet protecting the surviving victim's privacy.

I do not apologise for the graphic detailed accounts of the attacks on the victims as these are all accurate and demonstrate the viciousness, callousness and depravity of the offenders. The facts were obtained from the original crime files now currently stored in the Major Crime archive stores based at Avon and Somerset Police Headquarters, Portishead and directly from my own memories as the investigating officer. Each of the cases reported on were known to me personally as I worked on them during the review, investigation and prosecution of offenders. I lived each job for several years and in most cases spoke directly to the victims and offenders, giving me an insight into the effect that the crimes had on both.

The names of all the rape victims have been changed to protect their identity and to preserve their privacy. The murder victim's details are correct. Some locations have also been changed for the same reason. I have chosen not to protect the identities of the offenders as they have no right to the same level of privacy. The cases can all be found on the internet and were in the public domain during the investigations and trial.

As is often the case in crime investigations, the majority of the suspects chose to go no comment during interviews with the police so their account, reasons and thoughts at the time of committing the offences have been based on the evidence alone. The offenders mostly pleaded guilty at court to their crimes but still chose not to give their account. On occasions, where the cases went to trial, the offenders continued to argue their innocence but were found guilty. If I have suggested that the offender may have been responsible for other crimes, then this is a personal viewpoint. No evidence yet has been found to prove this to be the case and no additional offences have been charged.

It is only the victims and offenders who truly know the facts of the case so on occasions I have given my interpretation of the events; please feel free to disagree with me and form your own views.

Contents

Forward

The Cold Case Team   2003

Twisted Tooth Sex Fiend
Chapter 1   Kath   1979
Chapter 2   Nigel Palmer-Batt   2004
Chapter 3   Debbie   1983

The Clifton Rapist
Chapter 1   Kathleen   1963
Chapter 2   Helene   1977
Chapter 3   Anna   1978
Chapter 4   Operation Argus   1979
Chapter 5   Ronald Evans   2005

The Creeper Rapist
Chapter 1   Janice   1991
Chapter 2   Marissa   1992
Chapter 3   Matthew Bailey   2004

The Railway Attacker
Chapter 1   Vanessa   1980
Chapter 2   Thomas Stewart   2005

The Monstrous Case of Rape
Chapter 1   Valerie   1983
Chapter 2   The Davis Brothers   2005

The Baptist Chapel Rape
Chapter 1   Samantha   1986
Chapter 2   Valentine Barnett   2010

Operation Rhodium

Chapter 1   Melanie   1984
Chapter 2   Reviews
Chapter 3   New Familial DNA

Preview of other books in the series

Dedication

Author Biography

The Cold Case Team

In the mid-1980s, British scientist Prof Sir Alec Jeffreys found a way of taking a sample of someone's DNA and converting the sample into a unique genetic fingerprint. He realised that these numeric profiles could become an even more powerful crime-fighting tool than fingerprints.

By 1995, the forensic science service in the UK had developed DNA testing of crime scene samples and were getting significant results in matching profiles with suspects. It was then decided that a National DNA database (NDNAD) should be established that would not only store the details of scene profiles but would also store and search for matches with offender DNA profiles. Initially only people arrested for offences of violence, sexual assaults and burglary were swabbed, their DNA profiles were established and soon the size of the database grew.

It was realised that not everyone's DNA was stored on the National DNA database even if they had murder convictions in the past. Laws had been introduced to allow the police to take DNA samples from people with specified convictions, so all police forces decided that they would visit their local prisons and take DNA swabs from prisoners convicted of murder. It was during this process that one Ronald Evans, who you will hear about later, was required to provide a DNA swab and his DNA profile was loaded onto the NDNAD.

Prior to the setting up of a force Cold Case Team, the undetected murders in the Avon and Somerset police force area had been periodically reviewed at key times. The reviews were triggered as forensic science techniques developed. The discovery of DNA was recognised as the most significant evidential tool since the discovery of fingerprints. The DNA testing techniques were a new science and developed quickly. Two of the force's undetected murders had been reviewed resulting in an almost full offender's DNA profile being obtained, namely the Melanie Road murder in Bath in 1984 and the murder in 1976 of Susan Donoghue. Although these offenders' DNA profiles were known, they had not matched any suspect profile on the national DNA database so sat there waiting for the suspect to be arrested for an unrelated crime. When the murder reviews were carried out, a small team consisting of a Detective Inspector or Sergeant, a Senior Scene of Crime Officer and a Forensic Coordinator were allocated the enquiry. They would commission any additional forensic work and then allocate additional enquiries to Detective Constables before submitting a review report.

I am often asked, what is a cold case? A case becomes 'Cold' when all reasonable lines of investigative enquiries have been completed and the case remains open and unsolved.

What makes a good cold case review officer? They should I would suggest be an experienced detective with many years' service in the police, who understands the historic policing methods as well as having a knowledge of how forensic techniques have continued to develop year on year. The officer needs to have investigated many categories of serious and major crimes, in particular murders and rape offences. The personal characteristics sought for a Cold Case Reviewing Officer are:

- An individual who is very meticulous and thorough in their gathering, assessing and collating of all the available evidence whether it be evidence already known or evidence that needs to be found.

- An individual who questions the accuracy of everything, does not accept anything on face value and seeks corroboration wherever possible.

- Someone who can work well alone but also happy to work as a team and liaise with other agencies in particular forensic scientists.

- A person who never gives up and continues to strive to bring offenders to justice even when the odds are stacked against them.

In 2003, the Avon and Somerset Constabulary decided that it needed to set up a Cold Case team to continue to review the 23 undetected murders dating back to 1947 and to identify and investigate any undetected stranger rape offences.

It was decided that the best place to look for suitably qualified staff was the Major Crime Unit that had been set up in 2002 to support the investigations into all murders in the force area. When this unit had been formed, four of the most experienced Detective Sergeants from the Avon and Somerset Constabulary had been taken away from District CID offices as their level of knowledge was required. All these Detective Sergeants had 20+ years' service, and had worked on many of the force's most complex murder investigations. Detective Sergeant Mike Britton had served most of his CID service working from Bath CID, he had taken a key role in the undetected Melanie Hall murder investigation. Detective Sergeant Andy Jenkins had worked on Trinity Road CID, considered as one of the busiest CID offices in Bristol. I had spent my CID service at various offices around the Bristol area and had been the case officer in the Jenny King murder investigation, considered as one of the largest investigations of its kind. The Jenny King murder is covered in another of my books titled 'The Murder Detective'. Detective Sergeant Steve Taylor had served in Kingswood CID office and worked on Operation React that was the forces response to dealing with historic child sexual abuse in care homes and detention centres.

Detective Inspector Phil Kennel from the Major Crime Team had been on the same intake as me when we joined the police in March 1977, we had never worked together over our years in the force, but I was his first choice to set up and run the new Cold Case Team. I was 45-years-old, a Detective Sergeant who had been in the police for 26 years and 19 of those had been as a detective. I was certainly still keen and had a good understanding of current forensic matters as well as the background to understand how historic investigations were conducted. The challenge for me was to identify all the undetected stranger rape offences pre-2003 that were recorded in the Avon and Somerset area and then to set about locating the historic paperwork. The offences were so old that they had not been managed on any computer system, but files of paperwork were stored away at various locations on different districts. They needed to be found before any reviews could be commenced. Having worked on many of the districts, I had some idea of the strange storage locations I would need to search. When I say a team, the cold case team was to consist of me with one detective, two investigators and an analyst. We together had to set about finding all the paperwork. My initial research had identified 1,800 potential case files that we needed to locate, and I created a spreadsheet listing the cases, dates and locations of offences, victims' details and forensic laboratory references. The spreadsheet was further developed by me to show when paperwork was located and when reviewed. I also recorded any further forensic submissions as they were commissioned along with the results.

Garages in Thornbury and Yate police stations, stables and garages in Staplehill police station, old unused cells in Bridewell police station, attics in Frome and Southmead stations as well as locked cupboards in places like Bishopsworth, Bath and Taunton were locations that many of the files were tracked down. Every station was visited, and the pile of case files began to mount. All the paperwork was taken to the Major Crime Review premises at Kingswood police station and placed in an unused locked prison cell. They would remain there for the initial review process but were later housed in an archive storage facility at Portishead Police HQ.

Once the gathering process was finalised, it was clear that some of the files we were looking for could not be found and may have been lost for good. It was known that some had been destroyed by overzealous members of staff clearing out offices to create space, others had been lost when the cells in the basement of Bridewell police station flooded, destroying vast quantities of crime files. At this point, it was only going to be possible to review the files that existed, but there was years worth of work ahead of us.

Strangely some files consisted of only one piece of paper, others a whole crate of documentation and in the case of a serial rapist in Bath involving mass DNA swabbing, a total of 123 crates were located.

The law changed in 2004 to allow the database to hold the DNA of anyone arrested for a recordable offence and detained at a police station. This resulted in people being swabbed for much minor offences including drink driving.

Operation Nutmeg was a national operation which was funded by the government, it was supported by legislation that gave the police powers to visit people previously convicted of offences under the sexual offences act and to require them to provide a DNA swab. Anyone who refused to provide the swab could be arrested and DNA taken by force if necessary. Avon and Somerset were very vigilant in tracking down those identified for swabbing. This process was intended to ensure suspect DNA profiles were on the DNA database for matching to crime scenes.

By 2013, the UK National DNA database held 4.8 million suspect profiles and each day the numbers increased.

Avon and Somerset was not the only police force to set up cold case teams to investigate undetected rape offences but they were one of the first to pilot the idea and as police forces nationally saw the results coming in, they visited me in Kingswood in order to learn how I had set about gathering data, tracing files and the procedures I put in place to conduct effective forensic reviews.

The Devon and Cornwall force set up their Cold Case team in 2011 so they were many years behind us.

The Government also monitored cold case results and decided to release further funds to the Forensic Science Service for them to review all the material they had in storage in the hope of identifying cases suitable for DNA forensic testing. This resulted in the Forensic Science Service setting up Operation Stealth which identified 10 to 15 cases in most force areas but in the Avon and Somerset constabulary, there were only two new cases. This was because the force had already carried out reviews on most of their undetected historic stranger rape offences and the two identified were investigations where the police files had been missing.

I think now would be a good time to have a look at a few of the cases that my team and I reviewed and the painstaking enquiries that were made in order to get the results.

When I initially agreed to set up the Cold Case Team, I had no idea how much pleasure this type of enquiry would give me. I was initially concerned that I may lose some of my skills at working on live murder investigations and for that reason, I reached an agreement with Inspector Kennel that I would continue to be deployed in incident rooms on live murders and that my time on the Cold Case team would be limited to six months and reviewed after that. The plan at that point was for Detective

Sergeants, Britton, Jenkins, and Taylor to take their turn.

The Twisted Tooth Sex Fiend

Chapter 1:

Kath – June 1979

Kath Thomas was only 21-year-old, she was pretty in a natural sort of way, she was slim but not skinny and had long mousy brown curly hair that came down over her shoulders. She always dressed in a smart casual manner, wearing a little makeup but not as much as a lot of her friends did. She preferred a small amount that brought out the blue of her eyes and a little blusher to give her that rosy fresh look. Kath had no specific boyfriend that she was interested in, but she was very popular with all the boys because she was so easy to chat to, always happy to listen and appear interested in what they were saying to her. She had left school at just 16 years of age; she was not interested in higher education but preferred the idea of earning money and saving up to travel the world. Her current plan was to get a job as a receptionist in one of the local dentist practices because she knew that she could earn more money than she currently did. Since leaving school, she had been working for her parents in their sweet shop on the corner of Potters Road, and Two Mile Hill Road, St George, Bristol. Her parents were hoping that, as she was their only child, she would eventually take over the family shop, but they were aware that she had other ideas. As a thanks for all her hard work, Kath's parents had refurbished the two-storey one-bedroomed flat at the rear of the shop and given it to Kath as her first place of residence. Kath insisted on paying her parents rent but they would only accept a token contribution. Mr and Mrs Thomas lived in nearby Fishponds in a tidy three-bedroomed semi-detached house. They were happy that Kath lived close enough should she need them but also understood that she enjoyed her own freedom. Kath was a chirpy girl who had a small group of close friends that would often meet on a Friday or Saturday evening and go into town to one of the city's night clubs.

On this summer's evening Saturday the 2nd of June 1979, Kath met up with her closest friend Joyce, who lived nearby in Kingswood. They both took a bus from Kingswood into the city centre, and they spent the evening firstly in a couple of bars in Park Street, Bristol and finally decided on finishing the night at the Mandrake night club. The two women stayed together all evening. Kath was not really a big drinker and had decided to stick to glasses of gin and orange. Kath liked the occasional cider or beer but did not like mixing her drinks and with money being tight she limited her drinking. Kath and Joyce were approached by two young lads in the night club and happily chatted about their plans for the future. The lads bought the girls drinks and the four were dancing together as a group to Boogie Wonderland as the night club DJ called the evening to a close. It was about 2am when they left the club, saying goodbye to the lads, planning to meet up again in the Mandrake on some future Saturday. The girls walked alone to the taxi rank in the city centre and as planned got a taxi home. They did as was their normal practice and took the taxi together to Joyce's house and Kath then walked the 10-minute journey alone to her flat.

The streets were empty and besides a few cars driving home, Kath didn't see anyone. Kath arrived home safely and let herself into the flat by the side door, this led straight into her kitchen diner, where she kicked off her uncomfortable shoes by the door and immediately went upstairs to her bedroom as she was feeling tired from a fun night out. She felt quite merry having drunk about four gin and oranges, but she was in good humour, looking forward to a lie in on the Sunday morning before going to her parents for a roast dinner.

Having visited the crime scene myself, I have always imagined her attacker loitering in a nearby street passing his time, maybe smoking. It is likely his attention was drawn to the upstairs light being switched on by Kath. He no doubt retreated into the bushes and watched. He could have seen Kath closing her curtains as we know there was a slight gap where they had not shut completely. From the gap between the curtains and the silhouette on the material, he would have been able to tell that the pretty young female he had just seen enter the house was getting undressed. He may have hoped to get a clear sight of her as she undressed so he would have stood in silence getting more and more excited at the prospect. Perhaps he was disappointed that he had seen very little when suddenly the bedroom light went out and that was the end of his free entertainment. It is not known how long he waited maybe another 10 minutes but once he was satisfied that she was asleep, he walked across to the flat door and tried the handle. The door was locked, and from what we know from the crime scene, he realised that a small transom window immediately to the right of the door was not tightly closed, he pushed at the window and sensed it was a little loose. With a couple of sharp blows, the catch to the transom window popped open and rattled against the glass as it swung loose. He was soon able to lift the catch by using a piece of stick and the transom swung open. He needed to grab hold of the open window as he hauled himself up onto the window ledge, then by squeezing himself headfirst through the gap, he was able to clamber into the room. He would have immediately realised that he was in the kitchen as he had to negotiate the sink which was on the inside directly below the window. The sink and draining board were full of crockery so he would have needed to lower himself carefully making sure that he didn't disturb anything or make too much noise as he wanted to surprise the woman in bed. Once inside he quickly found the stairs leading off the kitchen. The stairway was only lit by the dim light of the moon shining through the window and although he could scarcely see where he was going, he silently crept up to the landing. Wanting to surprise his prey, he chose not to turn on any lights. I can imagine him moving slowly along the corridor unable to stop the floorboards from creaking gently beneath his feet. There were only two doors leading off the landing, but he knew from what he had seen when outside, which room the pretty young woman was going to be in, hopefully tucked up in bed fast asleep. Entering the bedroom, the sound of the door hinges squeaking would have appeared to be loud enough to awake the whole street, but Kath lay totally still breathing gently, totally unaware of his presence. He stood directly above Kath. His eyes became accustomed to the darkness, there was enough light coming from the street outside due to the badly drawn curtains.

We don't know how long he stood there watching Kath peacefully sleeping, transfixed by the rising and falling of her chest as she slept naked in bed only partially covered by just one white sheet. The bedding was only covering Kath from the stomach down, so he gently sat on the bed I guess, intending to take in the view he had of her body. Kath subconsciously felt something as he started to tug carefully at the sheet making it slowly descend and it was just as the sheet got down to her thighs that Kath began to stir and opened her eyes. It took a couple of seconds for her eyes to adjust, enough time for him to place a hand across her mouth and tell her to remain silent. He told her he had a knife and if she made a sound, he would kill her. All that Kath could do was to lie there and allow this man to totally control her. He teasingly pulled the sheet further down, little by little, each time exposing a little more. He continued and removed the sheet totally from her body until it was no longer concealing anything. Kath now lay fully naked and had to endure this man's hands as he explored her body. She could tell that he was clearly aroused, she could see from the swelling in his trousers, but she was just helpless to stop what was inevitable. The rape itself was very rough and quick, he could hardly restrain himself. Kath had kept her eyes tightly shut to blank out the full horror of what was happening, she had not even seen him remove his clothing. Once he was satisfied, he quickly pulled his pants and trousers back up and lent forward next to Kath's ear and whispered "*Thanks. You just lie there for ten minutes; I'll be downstairs listening.*" She could smell a sickly stale tobacco on his breath, and it clung in the air as he left the room.

Everything went silent until Kath heard a short clang sound which she recognised as the kitchen transom window catch. She had been having problems with it for weeks and had promised herself long ago that she would get it fixed. Kath lay there sobbing for quarter of an hour and then decided that she had to do something. She got dressed putting on a clean pair of knickers, jeans, and a jumper, she left by her flat door and just ran all the way to Joyce's house. When Joyce answered the door, Kath burst into tears and told her the whole story. Joyce persuaded her that the attack had to be reported and she called both the police and Kath's parents. Kath's parents were the first to arrive followed by the police about ten minutes later, both getting there within half an hour. Kath had to relive the whole attack again in detail and sign a 15-page statement. She underwent a medical examination, having intimate samples taken. She surrendered all the clothes she put on immediately after the attack in case any forensic evidence had transferred onto them. The police scenes of crime officer attended at her flat and worked out that the man must have gained entry and exited via the transom window. Dusting the area with silver fingerprint powder, he lifted a set of inverted finger impressions. These were typical of marks left by burglars as they entered properties and would be difficult to explain away as having been left there in any innocent way. These prints could be used to identify the offender and eliminate suspects. The prints were checked against all stored fingerprints of local burglars and sex offenders but were not identified. The offender had never had his prints taken before.

The Forensic Science Service found traces of semen on Kath's vaginal swabs and on the knickers that Kath put on after the attack and had worn during the run to Joyce's house. There was no such thing as DNA in 1979 and the semen was examined to establish a blood grouping of the offender. Any blood grouping would be helpful to eliminate suspects but could never be attributed to one individual. Unfortunately, the blood grouping found was not rare and matched sixty per cent of the male population and although useful, it would not be able to identify the offender.

Kath was asked to create a photofit of her attacker but found the process too difficult. Having to choose a specific set of eyes from fifty possible sets or a nose from fifty different noses was impossible for her, so she was asked to work with an artist to produce a sketch. There was one feature that was embedded in Kath's mind from the limited view she had of the man. She was convinced that the man had something unusual about one of his front teeth. It was either chipped, discoloured, missing or twisted.

Sketch prepared at Kath's direction

There was significant media coverage about the rape describing the attacker as a twisted tooth sex fiend. Any name suggested by the public was followed up but most were eliminated, either through the fingerprint or the blood grouping. Ten months later the case was filed as an unresolved cold case. Kath was so traumatised by the attack that from that day on, she never returned to her flat. She moved back in with her parents for many months. When she eventually found new accommodation and was brave enough to live away from home again, she was so worried about living alone that she always needed to take in lodgers to ensure that she was never sleeping alone in her house. Kath found it very difficult to form any sexual relationship with a man and the slightest thing would bring back memories of that night. Kath could not watch any programme on television that showed scenes of sexual intimacy, turning off the television or simply leaving the room to avoid having to explain herself to anyone else present what she had been through. Kath also found that certain sounds or smells sent her into a panic as they brought back images of that night in 1979.

News article referring to the attacker as the 'Twisted tooth fiend'

Having gathered together all the undetected stranger rape offence files in 2003, the very first case that I picked up to review was the burglary and rape of Kath Thomas in 1979 in Potters Road. I had located the paperwork in the garages at Staplehill Police Station where they had been slowly gathering dust. I had to wear a mask when doing my reviews as the dust circulating in the air would make me cough. As this was the first case, I designed a form to be used for all the individual reviews which would summarise the findings and assist when the process was repeated in the future. I felt it was important to learn as the review process progressed. The initial idea was for cases to be reviewed and additional forensic work commissioned. The victim and key witnesses would need to be traced and if a suspect was identified, he also had to be traced. We decided we would not contact a victim unless a suspect was discovered to avoid raising their hope of an arrest only to let them down. The plan was for the cases to be returned to district CID for the suspect's arrest and interview, but I argued strongly for the cases to be dealt with by the cold case officers to not only learn some of the pitfalls in dealing with a cold case, but I also felt my team should be allowed to see the case through to its conclusion.

Chapter 2:

Nigel Palmer-Batt – October 2004

The Kath Thomas case proved interesting right from the start. Remembering how policing had been in 1979, I knew how to carry out an initial quick scan of the documentation to find the information that I needed. I wanted a summary of the case, details of what forensic and scientific evidence had been gathered at the time and any forensic results. I would carry out the more detailed assessment of the file later.

Although the idea of reviewing was to consider any forensic testing that could now be done to obtain a DNA profile of the offender, I quickly realised that there was key fingerprint evidence in this case. The fingerprints lifted from Kath's kitchen window had never been identified and if they could be located at the HQ Fingerprint Department, they could now be checked again using modern science. One phone call to the HQ Fingerprint Department confirmed that the fingerprint lifts were still held in storage, where they had been placed in 1979. I knew about the introduction of the National Automated Fingerprint Identification System (NAFIS). This was a computerised system which enabled you to nationally check a fingerprint against the millions of sets of criminals' prints taken on arrest. NAFIS had been introduced in 1997 but had only reached all forces including the Avon and Somerset in 2001.

Fingerprints had been used in the detection of crimes as early as 1892 so it was not a new science, but the computerised system made comparison effective, and prints could be checked nationally. Once the computer detected a potential match, a fingerprint expert takes on the responsibility to confirm identification and provide evidential proof. I established that the scene fingerprint lifts were suitable for loading onto NAFIS and it could be done that very evening, with results being reported the following day as the computer carried out its checks overnight. In 1979, the fingerprints comparisons had been limited to a fingerprint expert comparing the lifted mark with local criminals and concentrated on burglars and sexual offenders, now NAFIS would be checking nationally against all fingerprints taken from all people arrested for recordable offences.

At 11am the following morning, I got the call I had been hoping for. The fingerprints had been identified as those belonging to Nigel Palmer-Batt. The fingerprint expert Derek Harvey had confirmed the identification, so I now had to start my research into locating Palmer-Batt. I soon established that Palmer-Batt was born in 1955 and at the time of the rape of Kath Thomas in 1979 had been living in the Hanham area of Bristol. Nigel Palmer-Batt had come to the notice of the police and as research continued, several interesting facts about him became known. He had previous convictions for football violence at the Ashton Gate football ground in Bristol, this gave an insight into his violent, aggressive nature. Palmer-Batt had a conviction in 1975 for indecent exposure in a public street in Keynsham. It is a widely reported fact that rapists have often committed minor sexually motivated offences prior to building up to a rape, offences such as theft of ladies' underwear or indecent exposure being quite common, so this discovery was not a surprise to me. It was just a shame that in 1975 Palmer-Batt had not been fingerprinted for the indecent exposure offence as he may well have been identified for the rape of Kath Thomas at the time. The most important fact that I discovered was that Palmer-Batt had his DNA profile stored on the NDNAD so if any offender's DNA could be found from Kath's intimate samples or clothing, this could be all that would be needed to arrest him. The fingerprint alone would not be enough to secure a conviction for rape albeit it could result in his arrest, and he would have a hard time accounting for the presence of his inverted fingerprints on the kitchen window in Kath's flat. I knew that any interview of Palmer-Batt would likely result in him answering 'No comment' to all questions so we needed to find more damning and supportive evidence.

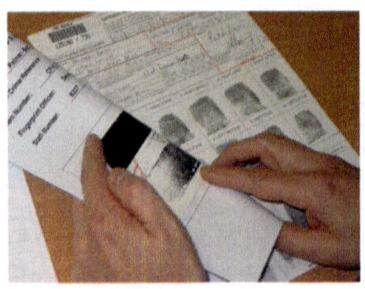

Manual checking of fingerprint

FINGERPRINT EXHIBIT

REGINA v   Palmer- Batt

Scene of Crime Reference: CP-61-79-B   03/5232

Item Number: CP-61-79-B   No 1

Fingerprint Officer: Derek Harvey

Staff Number: 8227

Fingerprint lift from Thomas crime scene

Palmer-Batt's DNA was on the DNA database because it had been taken in unusual circumstances. He had been working as a pianist on a cross-channel ferry in 1997 and had been subjected to a random check by customs officers who were searching staff looking for anyone smuggling contraband. When he was searched, he was found in possession of several homemade video tapes. They were viewed and they showed him having sex with different women, all of which appeared to be unconscious. Enquiries at the time had identified two of the women. When the women were shown the recordings, they were shocked, they had no idea that they had been abused in that way and were certainly not consenting. They were so embarrassed by the assaults that they stated that they would not support a prosecution or go through the court process but agreed for him to be cautioned. Palmer-Batt admitted the offences of administering substances to the women in order to stupefy them before he committed sexual acts against them, he also admitted to separate offences of indecent assault also depicted in the video recordings. He was cautioned for his crimes and, more importantly, his fingerprints and DNA were taken for loading onto the national databases. Palmer-Batt was sacked from his employment with the ferry company and chose to move away from the area to start his life over again.

DNA evidence was now needed in the Kath Thomas rape case and enquiries with the Forensic Science Service confirmed that they still had Kath's knickers in storage. They agreed to submit these for DNA analysis and stated that any result would be known in about five weeks.

The five weeks felt like an eternity to me and although the focus had changed from background research to tracking down Palmer-Batt, it was a positive forensic result that I so desperately needed. It was almost five weeks to the day that the fantastic news about the DNA test result was phoned in to me. Semen traces had been found on Kath's knickers; they had been the clean pair that she had put on immediately after the rape, so the semen had to be the attacker's. From the semen, the scientist was able to obtain a full DNA profile which they had already loaded onto the National DNA database, and this had matched the DNA profile of Nigel Palmer-Batt. I now had the evidence I needed. There were both Nigel Palmer-Batt's fingerprints at the point of both entry and exit at Kath's flat and semen found on her clean knickers put on after the rape. I knew that Palmer-Batt, when confronted with all the evidence, would either admit the offence, go "*no comment,*" or claim the sexual intercourse was a consensual act. I was convinced that any defence of it being a consensual act could be refuted due to the location of the fingerprint. Now it was a matter of tracing and arresting him.

Before arresting Palmer-Batt, it was necessary to make the difficult approach to Kath, to rake up the past for her and let her know that her attacker had been identified. Kath was not difficult to trace as she had never married so was using the same surname and still lived locally. Kath remained very calm when the news was broken to her and took no persuasion to support the police with the prosecution. She explained that since running from her flat to get help from her friend Joyce, she had not stepped foot in the flat again. The attack on her had scarred her for life and once her attacker was locked away behind bars, she would feel much better. Kath was also able to provide Joyce's contact details as the two were still good friends. Joyce would be key in providing support for Kath should a trial be necessary.

I discovered that Palmer-Batt was still employed as a pianist and was now working on a different cross-channel ferry, which belonged to a different ferry company from the 1997 one when he had been arrested with the video tapes. This was very concerning and there could be no delay in arresting him as he was potentially still a danger to women. He was living in northern France with a young French woman, but he travelled weekly between France and England on the ferry. The most straight forward way of arresting him would be to await his arrival at Portsmouth docks so he would be arrested on English soil. Plans were put in place and me, with three colleagues from the Cold Case Team, travelled to Portsmouth in October 2003 and stood at the dockside watching the ferry moor up. The captain was excellent and stopped anyone leaving the ship until we had located Nigel and arrested him. Nigel said nothing when cautioned but the look on his face when the reason for his arrest was explained to him was great to see. He obviously thought he had got away with his past offending and it was all now coming back to haunt him.

I decided to search Nigel's cabin looking for any historic photographs that could assist the investigation. Kath had produced a great artist impression of her attacker, but it looked nothing like the man who was now standing in front of me so old photographs may help in any disputed identification. It was creepy to see a video recorder positioned on the top shelf of a wardrobe in the cabin, it was pointing downwards towards the bed and there was the remote control for the camera on the bedside cabinet along with six packets full of prescribed sleeping tablets in the drawer. They may have been prescribed to Palmer-Batt, but they had been collected in England, Spain, and France during the previous week. No-one needed that quantity of sleeping tablets and I was concerned that Nigel had been up to his old tricks of drugging women for sex. The wardrobe revealed homemade video recordings, these were all seized and would require watching later. My colleagues and I returned to Bristol with Nigel under arrest and as soon as he was detained in a police cell we quickly scan viewed the video tapes and were shocked by what we discovered. Palmer-Batt was clearly in the centre of the shot lying on his cabin bed, with remote in hand he was zooming in on his groin region as if rehearsing what was to happen later. There were other clips which showed passengers on board a ship, they were all females and the operator of the camera was zooming in on the ladies' breasts or groins, enlarging the images as much as possible and leaving little to the imagination. He had clearly not changed his ways but none of the videos showed unconscious or drugged females so hopefully further offending had been prevented.

I arranged for Nigel's home in France to be searched for any evidence of his offending and for his girlfriend to be spoken to in case she was also a victim of Nigel's sexual deviancy.

Nigel's girlfriend did not make any disclosures to the police.

The ferry companies were made aware of Nigel's offending history and assured the police that they would change their recruiting processes to prevent situations like Nigel's ability to move from one company to another after being arrested for committing sexual offences.

In interview, Palmer-Batt claimed that in 1979 he would often visit Bristol city centre and pick up one-night stands. He claimed that he never had any problems with ladies and often had sex on the first night. He stated that he had never had sex with any female without consent. He believed he could recall the incident in St George because it was around his birthday. He claimed to have met a female in town and because she was out with friends, planned to meet up later near to her address. He had later met her again in St George and she had taken him to her flat which was at the rear of a shop. They had entered by the main shop door he stated. He could not recall what the shop sold but claimed that having walked through the shop they passed through an adjoining door to the kitchen area. He then went upstairs with the woman, and they had consensual intercourse before both falling asleep. Palmer-Batt said that when he woke up, he did not wish to disturb the young lady, so he went downstairs and let himself out. When he was asked to explain his fingerprints on the kitchen window, he went on to explain how he believed it would have looked suspicious leaving the building in the early hours of the morning via the shop door so chose to exit via the window instead (Less suspicious!! I don't think). Palmer-Batt was taken in handcuffs to Kath's old address by me and Detective Constable Peter James, a detective who was the interviewing officer. When we parked outside, he confirmed that the shop was the location that he had earlier referred to in interview.

Palmer-Batt did admit, that during one of his football fights in 1979, he had chipped his front tooth and needed dental treatment to sort out the problem. Kath had been right when describing her attacker. She would not be required to identify him now, but he was intending to fight any prosecution by claiming it was a consensual act between Kath and himself.

Palmer-Batt was charged with the rape of Kath Thomas and pleaded not guilty. He stood by his lame story throughout the trial. Kath and Joyce both attended court, to give evidence. Kath was so clear and certain about the details of her rape; she was clearly living the horrific attack one more time and fought off any suggestion that she had consented. The defence could not budge her from her account so had to leave it up to the jury to decide. They took only fifteen minutes to find him guilty of rape. He was sentenced to eight years imprisonment on the 19th of October 2004. In court Kath walked up to Pete and me, to thank us for believing in her and for never giving up our fight for justice. She was determined to now move on in her life in the knowledge that her attacker was no longer walking the streets of Bristol.

Nigel Palmer-Batt as he looked in 1979

      That was not the end of the police's dealings with Nigel Palmer-Batt. As other police forces started cold case investigations, he was later identified as a suspect once again but this time by the Devon and Cornwall police.

Chapter 3:

Debbie – August 1983

It was August 1983 and it is believed by the police that the offender had spent two hours walking through the residential streets in Quintrell Downs near to Newquay. It was a quiet village with very few people around and maybe the offender wanted to get to know the area well. He needed to know all the possible escape routes so that he could leave the area unnoticed, should he get disturbed. He walked slowly along Bridle Way and thought it would suit his purpose perfectly, there were plenty of trees to conceal his presence and, although the houses were mainly bungalows, it looked as though it was a good mix of middle aged and elderly occupants. He could easily have already stopped and loitered in bushes during that evening to stare into bedroom windows to see the curtains being drawn and the room lit up. He would only make out silhouettes and movements, so would have needed to rely upon his imagination to form pictures in his mind. He stood there in silence, smoking to calm his nerves. This appeared to be the MO (Modus Operandi) that he favoured prior to attacking his victims, the same MO that he had used in St George back in 1979.

Debbie White was 21 years old but looked much younger than her age, she had spent that August evening at her friend's house in the village of Quintrell Downs. They had been watching television and drinking and it had become quite late without them noticing. Debbie realised it was past midnight and her parents would be getting worried. She phoned them and told her father that she would be leaving straight away, and he offered to give her a lift home. Debbie insisted that as the walk home would only take her about fifteen minutes, she would be alright, it was a pleasant warm evening, however she was still happy when her father said that he and her mother would stay up until she got in. Debbie had walked the same route home on many occasions and she happily headed off along Bridle Way.

I don't believe it had been his plan to attack anyone in the street but was carrying a knife with him bearing in mind his previous experience in threatening women in the past.

He was surprised as he saw Debbie walking down the street and it was obvious that she would pass right in front of his hiding place. He let her pass within feet of him, she had no idea of his presence. As she passed, he pounced and flung his arm around her chest and the other across her shoulder so he could cover her mouth with his hand. He told her not to shout, that he had a knife, and he would kill her if she didn't walk with him. Debbie was taken across the road to a field and dragged to a secluded spot where she was made to lie on the ground. Debbie was wearing a skirt, which he lifted above her waist and her knickers were then torn from her body, she could smell the stale tobacco on his breath, and this was a smell that would stay with her for the rest of her life. The man both digitally penetrated her and at the same time he was kissing and licking her neck and cheeks. He lifted her t-shirt and began to fondle and kiss her breasts. Debbie remained motionless, terrified of being killed if she fought back. She then heard a dog barking, coming from a nearby garden and the owner calling for the dog to come inside. With this commotion, her attacker got up, told her to remain still and silent for ten minutes and ran off, across the field and back into Bridle Way, away from the houses. He was soon on his planned route back to his car and away from the area. Debbie waited about two minutes and as everything was silent, she dressed herself quickly and was home about five minutes later. Her mother and father were there to greet her but were shocked at the state she was in.

Her clothes were dishevelled and covered in mud. It took a further ten minutes before she could stop sobbing uncontrollably and explain what had happened. The police attended to take report of the indecent assault, but a search of the area proved unsuccessful. Debbie was medically examined with swabs taken from her neck, cheeks and vagina. Her clothing was seized and bagged up and submitted for forensic examination. The scientists found saliva on Debbie's neck and bra believing it to be the suspect's as it was male saliva of matching blood grouping. No offender was ever identified, and the case was filed eight months later as an undetected sexual assault.

I first became aware of this case when I received a phone call from the Devon and Cornwall Cold Case Team in 2014. I was working in Blackpool having teamed up with Mike Britton, who was by this time also a retired Detective Sergeant with experience on cold case work, having taken over from me. We were travelling the north of the country swabbing individuals to eliminate them from another cold case investigation about which I will give details of later. It was whilst in Blackpool having carried out five swabs and due to swab one more person before calling it a day, that I received the phone call. They had been working through their cold case rape offences and had submitted various exhibits for forensic testing in relation to the serious sex attack on Debbie White. They had just received back news of a DNA hit for Nigel Palmer-Batt. I knew the detective who phoned as I had met him several times at the regional review officers conference. The detective explained that the female had been walking home and was dragged into a field to get her off the road and she was subjected to a serious sexual assault before her attacker threatened to kill her if she called for help. He had run off following the assault. I obviously knew all about Nigel Palmer-Batt and was able to fully brief up the officer from the Cold Case Team. I gave him all the information that I felt would be useful to him to assist in preparing for Palmer-Batt's arrest and interview.

The law had changed in 2003 when Part III of the Criminal Justice Act was introduced allowing the admissibility of bad character evidence into trials. This meant that a suspect's previous behaviour and convictions could be put before a jury before they decided on a defendant's guilt. Whilst sitting on the promenade wall looking out to sea in Blackpool, I discussed the various aspects of bad character that we could supply to support the prosecution of Palmer-Batt for the assault on Debbie White. The evidence in relation to the rape of Kath Thomas might just about be enough to convince Palmer-Batt to plead guilty rather than force another trial.

The victim, now 53, was traced by the Devon and Cornwall police and fully co-operated with the investigation. She was keen for her attacker to be prosecuted.

Nigel Palmer-Batt, at the age of 61, was arrested and gave an initial no comment interview, he was charged with indecent assault and bailed to attend court. The evidence eventually convinced him to plead guilty at Truro Crown Court and he was jailed for 18 months. Finally, justice had caught up with Palmer-Batt yet again, following the review by Devon and Cornwall Police's Criminal Case Review Unit.

Nigel Palmer-Batt in 2014

Detective Chief Inspector Sharon Donald from Cornwall's Public Protection Unit said: *"The sentence reflects the guidelines available to the Judge for this particular type of offence committed in 1983. Today the same offence would attract a maximum sentence of life imprisonment"*.

"I'd like to pay credit to and thank the victim who has demonstrated great courage by assisting the investigation team in sending her attacker to prison."

The Clifton Rapist

Chapter 1:

Kathleen – November 1963

For the next series of attacks, it is necessary to set the scene by going all the way back to 1963.

You could hear the Beatles wherever you went back in 1963 and the youth of the day loved the music scene. Kathleen Heathcote was a pretty 21-year-old woman who worked as a shop assistant in Mansfield and had been saving up for months as she was planning to get married the following year. She was in a happy mood having discussed her wedding plans with her boyfriend, John Whalley a local miner.

That cold winter evening, on Thursday the 21st of November, Kathleen left her boyfriend's house in Selston and was intending to travel the six miles home by bus. She was in a great mood as many of the wedding plans were now agreed. It is known that she got off the bus at the Mansfield stop at about 11:00pm. She was wrapped up warm although it was raining and she expected to get a little wet for the final walk home. She was wearing tights, a long dress and a thick overcoat. She had on sensible flat shoes and her umbrella was up protecting her from the rain. She was happily walking along singing quietly to herself 'She Loves You'.

Ron himself was only 22, he was a handsome man, 6' tall, stocky build with a full head of long wavy brown hair. He worked as an electrician at his local colliery. Having finished work, he had been out for a few drinks at the colliery dance and then decided to drive the eight miles home. It was pouring down with rain and he was so lucky to be the proud owner of a blue Ford Cortina Mk 1.

Ron lived with his wife, who was pregnant at the time and with his mother-in law in a modest 2-bedroomed terraced dwelling in Brunner Avenue Mansfield, he really was not looking forward to getting home. Things had not been running too smoothly at home and he and his wife had had another argument that morning about how they never had any time together and their sex life being non-existent. He was sure the argument would start up again as soon as he arrived home.

It was then that he saw Kathleen in his car headlights, she was walking slowly along, getting soaked but still with a smile on her face, he could tell that she was singing to herself. Ron pulled up alongside her and asked her if she wished to have a lift home to get out of the rain. She was only about 200 yards from her home in Princes Street so she declined and explained that she would be fine, she then continued to walk across an area of common ground not noticing that Ron had jumped out of his car and was now following her, gaining ground quickly. She had only walked about 100 yards when she felt a hand grab her by the right shoulder and she was spun round. Kathleen could not scream as she felt his hand across her mouth and then a blow to the head. She put up a struggle but eventually collapsed to the ground unconscious. She was forcibly dragged to his car and placed in the rear seat, feeling dazed, confused and weak, unable to escape. Ron drove to nearby Skegby lane a secluded spot where he intended to have sex with her. He noticed a piece of waste ground set just off the main road. He drove his car across the ground over by the trees and stopped alongside the waste tip. Ron pulled Kathleen from the car, she was slightly more alert now and tried to fight him off, but her belongings were strewn over the ground as Ron attempted to hold her down to rape her. Kathleen would not surrender to this man and continued to fight resulting in him beating her several times about the head until she lost consciousness again. He could still hear her groaning and quickly realised the dire situation he was in. Ron used all his strength to pick up Kathleen's limp body and place it in the boot of his car. He looked around in the dark and could see her belongings scattered on the ground and collected everything he could find. He put some items in his jacket pocket and others he left on the rubbish tip. Ron then sat in his car for a minute or two to calm his excitement before starting his car engine.

It is not known what Ron was planning to do with Kathleen but whatever he intended rapidly changed. As Ron tried to pull away, the tyres simply spun in the wet mud and there was nothing, he could do to get his car moving, he had to think quickly, he had a body in the boot of his car.

Was she alive or dead at that moment, no-one knew. He was expected home soon but his car would not budge.

Ron decided to get a taxi home and once there he behaved as if nothing had happened. He claims that he skipped work and returned to his car the following day and it was only then that he realised on opening the car boot that she was dead.

Ron phoned for a recovery vehicle to attend and sat in the car to await its arrival. He had been there for quite some time and when no truck arrived, he sat thinking what he should do. A police car arrived at the kerb side and the policeman began to walk across the grass towards the car, Ron jumped out and approached the officer. Ron explained that he had been driving home and desperately needed to urinate, so had driven up on the grass area to be out of sight of the public to relieve himself only to realise that he was now stuck in the mud. The two of them walked across to the Cortina but despite several attempts could not budge it. The officer offered to take Ron to a nearby garage where he could arrange for a breakdown recovery. Ron thanked the officer, but before even reaching the police car a breakdown truck drove by and they flagged it down. The officer drove away leaving Ron and the breakdown driver to deal with the recovery. Ron paid the breakdown driver, got in his car and drove straight home, parking up outside his house.

He couldn't do anything with the woman yet as his wife was expected home soon and he wanted to be there. He had a quiet evening in with no rows and at about 7pm he took his wife and mother-in-law in the car to bingo. It was, at last, the opportunity he had been waiting for. Ron drove out to High Peak in Derbyshire where he pulled up in a quiet spot alongside Ladybower reservoir. He could now check on the woman in the boot.

Ladybower is a man-made reservoir that had been created in 1944 following the villages of Derwent and Ashopton being demolished and purposely flooded to make way for the much-needed water storage facility. Water levels have occasionally over the years, dropped sufficiently to reveal the secret streets and ruins of Derwent.

When she died is unclear, it was probably before he even placed her in the boot, but Ron would have you believe it happened over night and was an accident. To make things more difficult for the police, he decided to strip the body of all clothing and to dump the body weighed down in the water. As for the clothing, he put it in a bag and threw it many miles away in a patch of woodland on the way back home. Ron returned home and sat smugly in his mother-in-law's armchair content that he had covered his tracks. He was cheerful and chatty when his wife and mother-in-law arrived home, he had already moved to the family sofa to avoid any argument with 'The dragon'. The ladies had no idea he had been out, they were happy as they had won at bingo and had bought fish and chips home for them all to share.

It was not until late on the 22nd of November that Kathleen was reported missing by her parents. It was very much out of character for her not to return home and they were convinced that she had come to some harm so reported her missing to the police. As time went on, area searches were conducted and Kathleen's watch, underwear, spectacles, hat, umbrella and false teeth were found by the police on the refuse tip at Skegness Lane. Mrs Heathcote, Kathleen's mother positively identified the watch and because the strap was broken the police were convinced that they had located the scene where she had been attacked.

The basic details of the incident were circulated to all stations and PC Mike Thomas phoned into the incident room to explain how he had assisted a man at that precise location on the day after Kathleen's disappearance.

It did not take the Detectives long to identify the man that PC Thomas had assisted, PC Thomas had the man's car registration number recorded in his pocketbook and the name of Ronald Evans as the registered keeper. They were soon visiting him at his home with a warrant to search it. Ron was alone at home when they arrived and confidently let them in. He stuck to the same story he had given PC Thomas about having a piss in the bushes. During the search of the house, officers discovered several items of Kathleen's property in Ron's jacket pocket. He had forgotten to throw them away with her clothing. Confronted with the evidence he confessed to killing and sexually assaulting her. Ron gave an unbelievable chilling account of what he claimed had happened, stating that the killing had been accidental, whilst intending to have sex with her. He explained that he placed his hand across her mouth to keep her quiet and she had lost consciousness but was still alive when he had placed her in the boot of his car. He said that he had intended taking her to the local hospital, and he wanted the officers to believe that he put her in the boot rather than the rear of the car out of fear for what it may look like if he was found with an unconscious woman sat alongside him in the car. He had panicked when the car got stuck and had taken a taxi home, leaving the woman alive in his boot. When he returned to the car the following day, he realised that the girl was dead. When the policeman approached him, he became very worried and it was only at that point that he had come up with the idea of disposing of her body. He agreed to direct the officers to where he had disposed of her clothing and to Ladybower reservoir where he disposed of her body.

Royal Navy frogmen took 9 days searching amongst the ruins of the sunken village of Ashopton, which was 132ft under water but they eventually located Kathleen's body.

Ron pleaded not guilty to murder but guilty to manslaughter at Nottingham Assizes court in March 1964. The jury did not believe his story and unanimously found him guilty of murder. He was given a life sentence and sent to prison. I certainly don't believe his story, but I will leave you to make your own minds up.

Ron decided very early on during his time in prison that he needed to get into a routine to survive his time inside. Mealtimes were set in stone and although the food was very basic, he realised that he would have to eat everything to stay healthy. There were regular periods for socialising with other inmates, but he had decided to have just a couple of trusted friends and to avoid contact with the rest. Ron also decided that he would take daily exercise doing press ups and sit ups and was soon fitter than he had been for a long time. Study was an option for inmates to avoid the boredom and Ron decided to study law. He was convinced that he had been convicted for the wrong offence and should only be serving a shorter sentence for manslaughter. He wanted to appeal his conviction and even considered representing himself.

It was the night times that were the most difficult, once the lights were turned out by the prison wardens, he could only lie there on his bunk thinking and eventually dreaming. I imagine that he initially dreamt about that night in Mansfield and how he wished things had not gone so wrong. I suppose he may even have felt a little remorse but was he more likely feeling sorry for by the fact that he had been caught?

Knowing the crimes he was later to commit, I guess that his thoughts and dreams soon turned to other women and what he was missing out on. His dreams probably started normally enough with him meeting a beautiful woman and the two of them happily chatting, eventually agreeing to drive to a secluded outdoor location to be more private and intimate. They would be lying together on the ground cuddling and kissing before happily engaging in pleasurable sex. In time, Ron may have become bored with his thoughts and dreams, not finding them exciting enough. The dreams could then have taken on a more sinister feel, where he would take the woman to a quiet location in the country and lie together on the floor. Possibly the sex became more and more aggressive with him being the dominant one. I wonder if he imagined the woman telling him to stop but he would restrain her, threaten her and even half choke her to make her submit. He could not live out his fantasies in prison so would have to rely on the thoughts of seeing and feeling the terror in his victims' faces. The reason I have come to believe that Ronald's thoughts developed in this way is because of his behaviour since his release.

In 1975, Ron was released from prison on licence, he had by this time become a totally different man. He was certainly much fitter and stronger, but had he also developed these dark visions of sexual encounters? He decided to move well away from the Mansfield area relocating himself in Bristol. He apparently lived a normal life in Bristol with now his second wife.

Ron spent his first two years of freedom in the Avonmouth area settling in by finding rental accommodation and getting a job as an electrician. He was also getting to know the area and making friends, becoming quite popular in his neighbourhood as he was chatty and friendly to his neighbours, offering to do free electrical repairs for them. He bought himself a bright yellow Ford Capri to get about in, this was his pride and joy. He could often be seen washing and polishing his car at weekends. He soon found himself homing in on the Clifton/Redland area which had a high proportion of students living in bedsits. Ron started by touring these areas and taking pleasure at watching the young female students walking home alone without a care in the world. Did he try and relive his prison dreams by watching these women and letting his imagination take over?

In 1977, Ron appears to have realised that he could no longer control his inner urges to attack young women in the street and to subject them to serious sexual assaults and rape. He used the Redland area as his hunting ground because he knew it so well and realised the numbers of possible vulnerable attractive young women who walked around alone at night. He probably thought that he could control himself enough to avoid murdering anyone, but he had to find a release for his sexual urges. He had likely convinced himself during his time in prison that the death of Kathleen Heathcote had been an accident, whether the jury believed him or not. He would now test himself and embark on a reign of terror by selecting his victims carefully and leaving the area immediately after his crimes. Avonmouth was only a short drive away and as long as he was careful, he felt invincible.

The next two cases have a link to Ronald Evans, although I didn't know the link at the time that the undetected crime files were found in the attic at Southmead police station. This attic had been specially adapted for the storage of old crime files and admin paperwork. There was a permanent wooden stairway leading to the locked attic, which inside consisted of a large area of shelving containing historic crime reports in year and numerical order. The police force had an obligation to retain old undetected rape crime investigation files and I entered the attic with a long list of crime files that I hoped to find among the shelving. Searching through all the paperwork, it soon became clear that the stranger rape investigations were normally the thicker files containing lots of investigation material. Occasionally, the files were so thick that they had to be stored separately in a locked room at the far end of the attic marked on the door 'Oversize cases'. What was annoying was when there was no trace of the file I was expecting to find and no explanation as to why it was missing. To review a case, it was essential to have a starting point.

Chapter 2:

Helene - November 1977

Between 1977 and 1979 the police were getting swamped with sexual assault and rape offences being reported in the Redland/Clifton areas of Bristol. The description of the offender appeared consistent, so it was believed that a serial offender may be responsible and that they were looking for one attacker. However, it is always risky to assume offences are committed by one person and so easy to include some crimes that are in fact not linked.

At 12:30am in the early hours of 10th November 1977, 21-year-old Austrian student Helene Baur was walking home in Grove Road Redland. She had heard about the 'Clifton Rapist' but it never entered her mind that she would ever be a victim. She heard absolutely nothing until she was grabbed from behind and felt her attacker's hands wrap tightly around her throat. They were just passing an enclosed electricity sub-station and she was forced by her attacker to clamber over a low wall into the waste ground surrounding the metal unit. She was made to lay on the ground and froze in fear of what this man was intending to do to her, she was terrified but did not want to make things worse by fighting back. Helene's whole aim was to survive and give him no reason to kill her. He started by holding her down firmly on the ground, sat across her legs, pinning her right arm down with his left. She saw him fumbling around the crotch of his black tracksuit trousers with his free right hand and she could suddenly see he had hold of his erect penis. He told her to open her mouth and then thrust his penis inside, almost choking her with the force he used. Having calmed down slightly, he told her to suck gently or he would hurt her. Helene obliged but was desperate not to excite him too much as the thought of him ejaculating down her throat made her gag. Ronald needed more from his victim so reached up under her skirt and slowly pulled down her knickers from the crotch, once they were below her knees, he forced her legs apart and using the weight of his body positioned himself between her legs as he penetrated her, causing her great pain. He also penetrated her anus causing excruciating pain. With his hand now over her mouth, she was finding it hard to breathe and was certainly unable to call out for assistance and had to lie there in silence until the ordeal was over. It lasted perhaps ten minutes, but she lost all track of time as she tried to blank out what was happening to her. She was later unable to even tell the police if her attacker had ejaculated or not. Ron escaped as quickly as he had arrived and was already home by the time Helene was telling the police about the attack on her. She underwent the unpleasant procedures of a medical examination, making a statement, surrendering all her clothing to the police and compiling a photofit of her attacker.

Helene's intimate samples and clothing were all sent to the Forensic Science Service for examination, and these disclosed the presence of semen on the vaginal swabs and Helene's knickers. The forensic evidence available at that time was only able to provide the attacker's blood grouping and it did match the blood grouping of the other 'Clifton Rapist' victims but on blood grouping alone, this meant it matched forty per cent of the male population. It could be used to eliminate suspects but would never be able to positively prove the identity of the man responsible. The police knew that unless there was an admission by a suspect or an identification by one of the victims following an ID parade, it would be impossible to prove a person's guilt of these horrendous crimes. The police could only hope that one or two of the victims would be able to pick out their attacker when he was eventually caught.

Photofit

Sex fiend clues

THE SEX attacker who seriously assaulted a 21-year-old girl in Redland Bristol, early on Thursday wore a blue tracksuit with one or more white stripes down each arm.

Police believe the attacker also wore heavy-duty denim trousers.

Detective-constable Ian Laken wore similar clothes in Redland yesterday afternoon in a bid to jog the memory of anyone who has seen the attacker.

Police have warned girls in the city's busiest land not to walk alone after work. Anyone who can help inquiries should contact Redland police station.

News article about attack on 10/11/1977

Chapter 3:

Anna - December 1978

Anna Soltys was a 20-year-old Polish student who was planning her return home to Poland for Christmas. At 3:15am on 16th December 1978, she was walking in Saville Road back towards her bedsit in Redland. Her mind was on her family but she did notice the yellow Ford Capri as it drove past her on the Downs. The driver looked across in her direction and she watched as the Capri drove down the road, turned around and passed her again. She felt a little uncomfortable but the Capri passed without incident. Some three or four minutes later, she heard the sound of quick footsteps as someone came up behind her and felt an arm as it encircled her body from behind. There was a hand around her throat in seconds and she felt herself being pulled around the corner to a small grassy area. Her attacker appeared very practiced in his ability to overpower her. She was soon forced to the ground. She felt his hand reach up into her blouse as he forced it inside the cup of her bra around her right breast, and then freed the breast from its restraint. He moved his face closer to her body and began to suck and kiss her breast concentrating around the nipple. She felt terrified about what was happening. He then turned his attention elsewhere and she noticed as she looked down at his right hand that she was looking at his semi erect penis in his palm. He physically forced her to open her mouth and entered her, she gagged twice as his penis moved in her mouth and at the moment of his ejaculation, she almost choked as the semen hit the back of her throat, he then moved his attention to her vagina as he was desperate to rape her. He had only succeeded in pulling her knickers down and forcing her legs apart when a sound in the distance disturbed him, he released his grip on Anna and ran off into the darkness. Ron was back in his car and driving to the safety of Avonmouth before the police had even arrived at the location.

Anna went through the same procedures as Helene had a year earlier. Semen found in her mouth swabs came back to the same blood group. forty per cent of the male population. She too provided a photofit.

Anna could not say with any certainty that her attacker was anything to do with the driver of the yellow Ford Capri that had paid her so much attention, but she told the police all about it in case it could assist in getting this violent man off the streets of Bristol. The police traced hundreds of yellow Capri owners but Ron Evans was not amongst them. He continued to work as an electrician during the day, attacking women at night and returning home to his wife and daughter who were oblivious to his crimes.

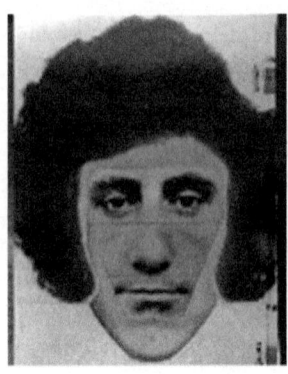

Photofit prepared by Anna

There were a number of photofits circulating the local police stations and in the media, all created by victims believed to be of the same Clifton attacker. There was quite a similarity between them. I was a young police officer working at Broadbury Road police station at this time in my service. In fact, I lived in two different bedsits myself in both the Clifton and Redland areas so was well aware of the fear this serial rapist was causing the public. The media reported the cases and explained the impact that these crimes had on the public. There were demonstrations in the street as young women felt scared to go out alone at night and the pressure put on the police to arrest the offender was enormous.

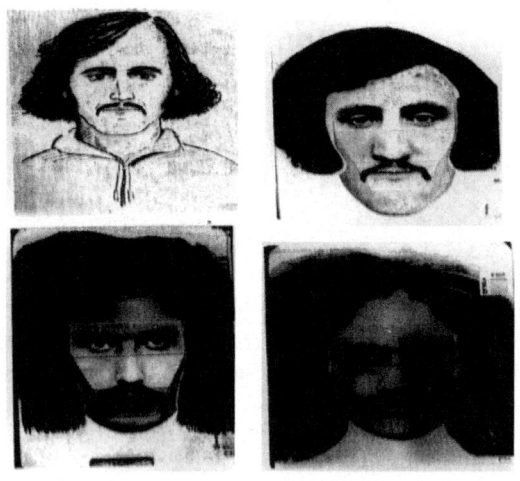

Photofit images of the Clifton Rapist

Chapter 4:

Operation Argus – March 1979

The police had already identified that many of the sexual assaults were the work of a serial attacker, and they were getting nowhere nearer to identifying the man so had to come up with new innovative ideas as to how they could identify and capture the culprit. An intricate decoy operation was put in place called operation Argus.

There had always been a reluctance to set up decoy stings because it meant putting police officers' lives at risk and the police were concerned that any decoy sting may be considered by some as a honey trap situation. If officers were going to be asked to walk alone up the main streets in Clifton/Redland in a hope that the attacker would pounce on them, it was going to be necessary to have backup immediately on hand.

The most likely target area for the attacker to strike was identified as being the roads running off Whiteladies Road in Bristol but this would mean decoy officers being asked to walk alone on both the main busy Whiteladies Road and several residential side streets. Female officers in plain clothes would be asked to walk along the street apparently alone but with colleagues concealed in bushes at strategic locations en-route. They would be in constant radio communication with each other, and it was planned to continue for as long as it took until the attacker was caught. Due to the cost of such an audacious plan, it was necessary to set a three-month cut-off date. The female officers were made aware of how violent the attacker had been and understood that if they were grabbed by him, it was likely that they would be taken to the ground before assistance arrived. The bravery of the women officers should not be underestimated. There was significant concern by senior officers in charge of operation Argus about young policewomen putting themselves in danger and due to the small numbers of young female officers in the force in the 1970's it was decided that male officers in drag would have to be used to boost the numbers. The officers were all given additional self-defence training by one of the male officer volunteers Constable Chris Gould, and he, along with his male colleagues, were given advice by the female volunteers on how to apply makeup as well as how to walk in a more feminine manner. This additional training proved very successful as many of the male officers found themselves being chatted up and pestered by men whilst on decoy duties walking the streets of Redland.

On 23rd March 1979, 23-year-old WPC Michelle Tighe was one of four officers being used for the decoy operation that evening. She knew the streets of Redland well as she had been patrolling them in uniform for two years. When the opportunity came for her to work alongside the CID on a decoy operation, she jumped at the chance. Operation Argus had been running for eleven weeks, and although it had resulted in ten arrests none were the offender they so desperately wanted to catch. Eleven policewomen and four police men had been used as decoys. This was about the 16th night that Michelle had been asked to work. She was a pretty female officer with a bubbly temperament. The weather was typically cold on this March evening, and she was dressed in long brown boots, trousers, blouse, a thick polo-neck jumper and black leather jacket. She wore a striped scarf to keep warm and carried her handbag over her right shoulder, which contained both her miniature police truncheon and radio communication equipment. She knew the circuit that she had to walk, in fact knew the layout of all the shop windows that she had passed so often.

She was about to start her 5th circuit that evening and knew that it would take sixteen to seventeen minutes, it had been normal to manage six or seven circuits per night. Nothing seemed out of the ordinary that evening and she felt the usual nervous excitement knowing that she was likely to be stopped once or twice by men asking for a light or inviting her to their homes for a night cap but the chances in her mind of her being targeted by the rapist were slight.

At 3am, Michelle was halfway through her circuit, walking up Whiteladies Road, Redland when the support team noticed that the occupant of a yellow Ford Capri was paying her a lot of attention. A PNC check was carried out on the vehicle, and this showed it to be registered to Ronald Evans, but more concerning to the officers carrying out the check, was the fact that enquiries into him showed he had a previous conviction for murder and was a life licensee.

The murder conviction relating to Kathleen Heathcote made chilling reading. The operation commander Kelvin Hattersley had the job of notifying Michelle over the radio that she had a killer on her tail because Ron had started to follow her discretely on foot. She was told that it was her decision if she wished to continue with the decoy operation or call a halt to it. She not only agreed but insisted that things should continue as planned. She could feel her heart pounding in her chest terrified about what could happen on the one hand but desperately wishing that the man would attack. The instructions to all the officers had been to allow the suspect to attack the decoy before breaking cover and making an arrest. This would ensure there was evidence of the offender's intentions and improve the chance of a successful conviction. The support officers were already in position, so Michelle turned off the main Whiteladies Road. Within two streets, Michelle could hear Ron increase his pace and was aware he was running up behind her. She chose not to look back as she did not want to scare him off. She knew any second now that his intentions towards her would be made clear. Michelle suddenly felt a force as he grabbed hold of her around her neck, he spun her around and pushed her violently towards the ground, she struggled with him to stop herself falling to the floor and hoping she could resist long enough for her assistance to arrive. She was able to shout out and had fortunately only received one back handed blow to the face before DC Andy Kerslake broke through the bushes and tackled Ron Evans to the floor. Ron was arrested for the series of all seven sexual assaults as well as the physical assault on Michelle.

Ron's blood group was quickly confirmed as being the same as the attacker's so at least that supported the evidence that he could be the serial offender that they were hoping to catch. When he was interviewed, he, like so often happened, replied "*No comment*" to all questions put to him. He was not going to provide that important additional evidence of admission needed. Several ID parades were conducted for those victims that believed they could identify their attacker, but due to the passage of time, none made a positive ID. Anna Soltys was the closest to making an identification but she could not be sure. Ron Evans was no doubt feeling more confident as each ID parade proved negative. The media were reporting the story about the 'Clifton Rapist' and the 'Beast of Clifton' being caught but there was still not enough to charge Ronald Evans with anything other than the assault on Michelle Tighe. He would go straight back to prison, having his life licence revoked but that was no satisfaction for the police.

Ron then made the unusual decision to ask to speak with the Senior Investigating Officer. He knew himself he was going straight back to prison to continue his life sentence, and he wanted to be allowed to speak with his wife before that happened, wanting to convince her that he was not the evil man being described in the media. Ron offered to admit to some of the offences if he was granted his wishes. He was told that any visit would be supervised but he would be allowed to see his wife. It was clear in his conversations with his wife that he wanted to tell her that he was not a rapist, he seemed happy to accept indecent assaults but the stigma of being a rapist was too much for him to accept. He also needed his wife to promise to stand by him.

Ron then went on to admit 5 of the sexual assaults in Redland. The offences he admitted were all classified as indecent assaults which had a maximum prison sentence of two years each. He refused to admit the rape of Helene Baur or attempted rape of Anna Soltys which both had a maximum sentence of life imprisonment. These two being the most serious attacks would remain undetected even though it was obvious to all those involved in operation Argus that Ronald was responsible.

Ronald as expected had his life licence revoked and was sentenced to a further nine years on top for the indecent assaults and assault on Michelle. He would certainly have been sentenced to a lot more time in prison had he been convicted of two rapes on top of the five indecent assaults.

Ron also received some credit for pleading guilty to the indecent assaults.

Image of Michelle Tighe dressed ready for decoy duties

PC Chris Gould and Robbie Jones dressed as a decoy for operation Argus

The unresolved cases of Helene Baur and Anna Soltys were filed as undetected cold cases. The evidence in the Soltys case involving the sighting of the yellow capri resulted in that crime report being filed along with the Operation Argus detected crime file.

There were some doubters at the time that the Helene Baur rape was one of Ronald Evans crimes because the photofit was not a strong enough likeness. It is for that reason that it was filed separately as an undetected rape offence and found by me amongst the 1977 crime files in Southmead attic.

Policewomen from operation Argus, with Michelle Tighe in the front centre

Photograph found of Ronald dated 1978

*Images of Ronald
on arrest in 1979*

Chapter 5:

Ronald Evans – May 2005

Having got matters underway regarding the Nigel Palmer-Batt investigation, I picked up the second set of cold case investigation papers, this time relating to the attack on Helene Baur. There was no indication that it had ever been considered as an offence that was part of a series. The file was fairly complete, and it was clear that semen had been found on vaginal swabs taken from Helene and on Helene's knickers. If these items could be located by the forensic science service, I knew there was a good chance that they could now be tested for the offender's DNA. The lab was soon able to confirm that they still had Helene's knickers stored in one of their freezers and they were given the authorisation to further examine them. The labs records indicated that the vaginal swabs had been returned to the police in 1978. Whilst waiting for the DNA results from the knickers, I searched every fridge and freezer within the police force to try and locate the vaginal swabs, this amounted to fifty-four appliances. There was no trace of the swabs anywhere, surely, they had not been thrown out.

Five weeks passed until I received a call from the lab confirming that they had a full DNA profile from semen on Helene's knickers and when the profile had been loaded onto the National DNA database it had resulted in a match to Ronald Evans. The scientist was a little surprised that the name meant nothing to me, the scientist knew that Evans was the infamous 'Clifton Rapist'. Although I was aware of the historic Clifton Rapist investigation, having been a young Police Constable in his probation in 1978, I had not been involved in such a major crime investigation. I needed to make myself fully aware of Ronald Evans' offending history.

I set about locating any of the files relating to Operation Argus. Operation Argus was considered a series of detected sexual assault offences so had not come under the radar of the cold case team before. The search for the Operation Argus paperwork took me back to both Redland and Southmead police stations. These stations were both on 'C' Division, where the Argus offences had been committed. When I had originally visited the loft at Southmead police station, I remembered the locked room at one end of the attic for the oversized cases and I had a vague recollection of finding a large cardboard box marked operation Argus, detected crimes. I had not looked inside at the time as detected crimes were of no interest to me but now, I needed to see the contents. In it, was the entire Operation Argus investigation along with the papers relating to the undetected attack on Anna Soltys. In a polythene bag, at the bottom of the box, were six long plastic sealed tubes containing swabs. These were labelled high, low and external vaginal swabs of Helene Baur. The decision to persist in the search had paid off as I now not only had the

Helene Baur swabs that I could submit for forensic testing, I also had another undetected crime relating to the Anna Soltys case to review. This was no longer going to remain a 'missing file' on my spreadsheet.

It was apparent from the Soltys case that oral swabs had been taken from her following the attack and because she had stated that the offender had ejaculated into her mouth, there was a chance of getting DNA evidence. I made a telephone call to the forensic science service to see if they could locate the mouth swabs taken from Anna in 1978. Within days, these were located in secure frozen storage at the laboratory. Unfortunately, the forensic testing showed that there were only five sperm head present on the swabs and still in 2003 the science required in the region of fifty sperm heads to obtain any realistic DNA profile. There was no forensic evidence to prove Evans was the offender, but the scientists were hopeful that at some stage in the future, forensic science would develop even further to make testing of so few sperm head a success.

Ronald Evans was traced and in fact was still detained in prison although he was due to be moved to Leyhill open prison in Bristol within the month. I immediately put a stop to this and arranged for Evans to be kept in a secure prison until a date could be fixed for his arrest. With Evans' offending history, it was not difficult to persuade the prison authorities that he was still a potential danger to women partially because he had not admitted all his crimes.

I went with my team to Channings Wood prison on 2nd March 2004 to collect Evans. He was arrested for the rape of Helene Baur and as is so often the case, he made no reply. He was further arrested for the rape of Anna Soltys and remained impassive. Evans sat quietly in the back of the police car for most of the journey from prison to the police station where he was going to be interviewed. He only spoke about how he had studied law, whilst in prison and believed he had a good case for a miscarriage of justice, he honestly believed he should only ever have been convicted for the manslaughter of Kathleen Heathcote rather than her murder. He was proud to claim that he was one of the longest serving prisoners in the UK even though he felt he should not have had a life sentence for the death of Kathleen Heathcote. Evans also spoke about having anger management classes in prison and felt his aggression was well under control.

Detective Constable Ian Calloway had been selected to conduct the interviews with Evans. Ian was an experienced detective as well as a highly trained interviewer. When Ian slowly put all the facts to Evans in interview, he claimed that he had not raped Helene but admitted that he had forced her to perform oral sex on him. To explain the semen found in her knickers, he stated that Helene must have spat out the ejaculate into her knickers afterwards. He was determined to only admit an indecent assault. He was behaving, yet again, as he had in March 1979 by only being prepared to admit indecent assaults rather than rape.

It was then explained to Evans that although the forensic evidence relating to Anna Soltys was not sufficient to prove he was the person who had ejaculated into her mouth, it was a similar MO to the offence he was admitting, she had seen a yellow Ford Capri immediately before her attack and he owned such a car. I suggested to his solicitor that Evans should think long and hard about admitting the sexual assault as it may be that he would be re-arrested in five or six years time, when forensic science processes would have developed enough to prove it was him. Evans through his solicitor was persuaded and he went on and admitted to the attack on Anna as well.

Ronald Evans was charged with the rape of Helene Baur and an attempt rape on Anna Soltys. These were the offences that the victims were claiming had taken place and I was not prepared to accept Evans claim that both were only indecent assaults. The law as it stood in 1979 stated that forcing a victim to submit against their will to oral sex was an indecent assault and I knew we would need to prove the rape on Helene and his intention to rape Anna.

In May 2004 the Sexual Offences Act 2003 came into force which changed the law relating to rape and the new definition of rape included penetration, no matter how slight, of the vagina or anus with any body part or object, or oral penetration by a sexual organ of another person without the consent of the victim.

Was there going to be the need for a trial in court for the jury to decide if Evans had only sexually assaulted Helene by forcing her to perform oral sex rather that an offence of vaginal rape as she claimed. The offences charged had to reflect the laws as they were in the 1970 and not current legislation.

In order to try and convince Evans to plead guilty to rape, I decided I would submit the vaginal swabs recovered from the locked room in the attic at Southmead police station. I knew there would be an issue regarding their integrity, continuity and poor storage. I was concerned that it was unlikely that they would produce any successful forensic result because the swabs had not remained frozen as was the best recognised method of long-term storage, but it was worth trying. The high vaginal swabs did in fact produce a full DNA profile of Ronald Evans and once he was served with this additional evidence, it was enough to convince him to plead guilty to Helene's rape. He also pleaded guilty to the indecent assault on Anna. Anna's views were sought regarding going to trial in a hope of proving the offence of attempted rape, but she was content with him being convicted of indecent assault to avoid a trial.

Ronald Evans was sentenced on 13th May 2005 at Bristol Crown Court to ten years imprisonment. His life licence was revoked for the second time.

When Helene had been told about her attacker being identified and about his admissions, she explained how the rape had affected her over the years. She had never bought a pair of high heeled shoes since as she always wanted flat shoes to be able to run off if in danger. She had formed the habit of walking down the kerb edge of pavements to steer clear of garden hedges. She had returned to Austria, her country of birth and never revisited the UK since.

Anna explained that the only place she felt safe was the small French village she now lived in, but she felt her trip back to the UK to sign statements for the case, although a massive challenge for her, did assist help her in moving forward. Both of these determined ladies were so relieved with the outcome and were able to thank me in person for tracking down their attacker and sending him back to prison.

One of many successes of the cold case team

I don't want to spend too much more time on Ronald Evans but you may be wondering what has happened to him since? In 2018, Ronald at the age of 77 appeared once again before the parole board for them to decide if he was safe to be released from prison or if he still potentially posed a danger to the public. They couldn't afford to make a mistake again. In 1975 he had been allowed out on life licence and had gone on to sexually assault seven women before his eventual arrest after operation Argus. In 2004 he was about to be transferred to an open prison prior to release. That was the last time I had direct contact with him, transporting him from Channings Wood prison for interview and I was of no doubt that he still had the potential to cause harm to women. So, in November 2018 the parole board having listened to his application decided that he could be released from custody on life licence with various conditions imposed including a requirement to take up residence in London and not to visit Bristol.

Evans had only been out of prison for a short time when ladies from his local community centre reported him to the police for offences of sexual assault. His MO was to befriend ladies who were aged 46 years and 53 years and invite them to his home address for a cup of tea and a chat. He would then use inappropriate sexual language and touch them over their clothing in a sexual manner against their wishes. Both victims were no doubt selected by him due to their physical disabilities making them quite vulnerable.

He was arrested on 12th of August 2022 and replied no comment to all questions put to him by the police. The only explanation he gave was to say "*I have treated both ladies with kindness and respect and the relationship is platonic with one lady and short and sweet with the other. Anything I did to these ladies was out of kindness. I tried to help them*". Evans was recalled to prison, for breach of his parole. A police investigation was carried out into the complaints made against him.

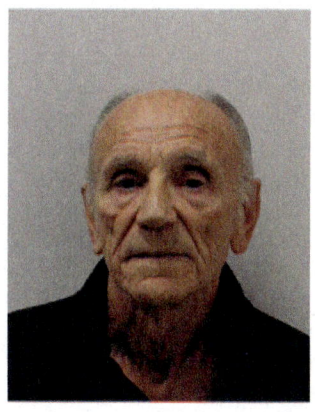

Photograph of Ronald Evans 2023.

In November 2023 due to structural damage at Harrow Crown Court Ronald Evans appeared at Hendon Magistrates court but it was for a Crown Court trial hearing in front of a judge and jury in relation to three counts of sexual assault. The offences were committed in 2021 and 2022 and they were relating to the two female victims previously referred to. Evans legal team explained how unwell he was, his 83rd birthday was approaching and he was reported to be on various medication and partially deaf. When he spoke in court however his voice was strong and clear not sounding the frail person his defence barrister had suggested he was. The trial lasted one week and the jury acquitted him of two offences but found him guilty of one offence of indecent assault. The judge was so concerned about Evans' previous offending history that she raised the tariff and sentenced him to 4 years imprisonment commenting on the concerns she had about the danger he posed to the public.

Ronald Evans is back in custody on his original life licence and surely there is no likelihood of any future parole board granting him his freedom.

I think it is important to point out that not all cold cases can successfully be solved, it just so happened that the first three files that I chose to review proved to be successful. Many of the cases reviewed had no forensic potential and were refiled in case new evidence came to light in the future or someone chooses to admit the crime. There were also a number of cold cases that contained some forensic evidence, but not sufficient to consider further forensic testing at that time. Each time samples are tested by the laboratory, some of the evidential material gets destroyed. Forensic techniques are developing all the time and it is important to know when it is worth taking the risk to conduct further testing.

Some of the cold cases reviewed were marked up for further reviews in the future when more sensitive DNA testing becomes available. The Anna Soltys case would have awaited further forensic developments in the future had Evans not chosen to come clean.

The next cases I have chosen to detail are once again an example where one offender was eventually identified as being responsible for two unconnected rape offences. The files were both located together in a storage room by the prison cells in Trinity Road police station. They had been filed together as they had been investigated as linked offences in 1991/1992. The offences occurred only 250 metres apart yet six months apart. As both attacks had occurred inside premises, which was an unusual MO the team investigating were convinced that they were linked.

The Creeper Rapist

Chapter 1:

Janice - June 1991

Janice Roberts was a 22-year-old woman but her past had been quite a sad one. At the age of 17 she was finding life very stressful, with boyfriend troubles and exams, she was feeling very low and depressed. Her father was sat watching rugby on television when he heard a thud sound coming from upstairs, he went up to investigate and immediately saw Janice on the landing, hanging from a ligature around her neck, tied at the loft entrance. A bedroom chair was on its side having been kicked over by Janice as she attempted to take her own life. It was clear she was still alive, her father cut the rope immediately and lowered her to the floor. He started CPR as his wife phoned for the ambulance and the police. Doctors discovered that Janice had not only tried to hang herself but had also taken an overdose of sleeping tablets. Janice was placed in an induced coma and was eventually brought round a week later. Janice survived her suicide attempt but at what cost! The oxygen had been starved from her brain and she was significantly brain damaged. Her parents tried to care for her at home but realised that her brain damage was too severe, and she had to be sent for permanent care at St Mathias Lodge in St Werburghs, Bristol, a residential care home for adults with mental health problems. Janice had become a popular resident at the care home and was known by all the staff and other residents. She had limited communication skills but could physically get about well and had her own room on the first floor next to the fire exit. She was a contented quiet young woman who spent her time mixing with other residents at the home and would go out on the occasional trip in the home's minibus. The home had strict rules, none of the residents were allowed outside unaccompanied but some would open the fire door and stand by the fire escape stairs to have a chat or a smoke.

Janice had qualified for her own bedroom due to the number of years she had been resident. The other residents had either single or double rooms and the first floor was limited to females with the males on the ground floor. Staff were present at all times and slept on the premises. The doors to the residents' bedrooms could not be opened from the inside to prevent the residents wandering around freely at night but could be opened by staff from the outside without the use of keys. This was to enable quick evacuation if necessary.

It was Saturday 22nd June 1991 and Janice was in her own room (Room 39) having gone to bed about 10:00pm. The time was now about 4:00am and staff were alerted to banging noises and footsteps coming from Janice's room. On approaching her room, they heard screaming and on entering found Janice lying on her side in bed. The bedclothes were pulled to the bottom of the bed and her night dress was pulled up exposing her bottom and thighs. Her face was bruised, and she was bleeding from the mouth. When she was helped to her feet, a used condom was found on the mattress beneath her. She was unable to explain to staff what had happened to her, who had attacked her and was clearly extremely traumatised. The police were called but could get no more information from Janice. Her lack of communication skills meant she could not provide a description of her attacker and her distressed state did not assist with trying to establish what had occurred. The police had to rely upon the physical evidence, it was obvious she had been the victim of a violent physical and sexual assault. The fire door next to her bedroom door was open so that was the likely point of entry and exit for any attacker. All the residents and staff were accounted for.

A medical examination was carried out by Police surgeon Dr Norfolk and this revealed fractures to both Janice's cheekbone and jaw as well as bruising to her face, collarbone, neck, knee and thigh. The condom (Exhibit AFH 1) was seized and later submitted for forensic examination.

The forensic scientists examined the condom and it was found to contain semen. The semen was blood grouped and the result assisted with elimination of suspects. Some of the male residents were tested with the knowledge of their families but all were eliminated. The police concluded that the offender was a burglar, having gained entry to the building by the insecure fire door, accidently left open by a resident. The person entered intending to steal and went to search the nearest room to the fire door. He fortunately or knowingly propped open the bedroom door or he would have been locked inside. Having attacked and probably raped Janice, he left the same way as he had entered. By January 1992 the case was about to be filed as an undetected cold case when the police were called out to another rape only 250 metres away in Waterson Road, St Werburghs.

Chapter 2:

Marissa – January 1992

Marissa Cromer was 21 years old and had only been married for 2 years. She lived with her husband in their newly purchased terraced house in Waterson Road, St Werburghs, Bristol. Marissa's husband worked nights driving taxis, so she was used to being alone. Marissa had gone to bed about 11:00pm on Saturday 5th January 1992. It was a cold winter's night, and she was wearing her thick nightdress. Marissa had been asleep for a couple of hours, but something disturbed her, she felt a cold breeze and looked across to her bedroom window and could see the shape of a man stood watching her. Her bedroom window was wide open. The window was above a flat roof from the outhouse which was obviously how the man had got in. The man demanded to know where she kept her money, she told him that she had none. She started to shout and hit out, so he pinned her to the bed as she struggled. He began to hit her several times with his clenched fist to the left side of her face and she could feel it swelling up immediately. He threatened to kill her if she did not do as he told her. He then instructed her to turn over face down on the bed and punched her again as she didn't react quick enough. The attacker then made her kneel up on all fours and grabbed her nightdress and hoisted it up over her head. Marissa felt totally helpless as she was aware that her buttocks were totally exposed to her attacker. She felt him trying to enter her, but he was having trouble as she squeezed her legs tightly together. He forcibly spread her legs further apart and then she felt him penetrate her and could sense him as he deposited his fluid within her. He did not realise it was this that would later prove his guilt. He was still not satisfied and made Marissa turn over and told her to suck his penis. She was still fighting him off when she blacked out and had no recollection of what occurred next until she regained consciousness at 5:00am and phoned the police.

Marissa was medically examined by Dr Hillary Cooling, an experienced police surgeon. The whole of the left-hand side of her face was swollen and bruised, and there was bruising to her right armpit and forearm, she had cuts to the inside of her cheek and was finding it painful to talk. Intimate samples were taken, and her nightdress and bedding were seized.

The vaginal swabs and nightdress revealed their evidence of the offender's semen. The similarities between the rape of Marissa and the attack on Janice were obvious, the level of the physical assault and the blood grouping of the semen confirmed that it was possibly the same offender.

The two cases were never detected and had to be filed later that year as cold cases.

They were kept together as potentially linked and filed in the cupboard at Trinity Road police station along with other undetected crimes.

Chapter 3:

Matthew Bailey – October 2004

Having had a number of unsuccessful reviews, I was looking for another case with potential. I then picked up the Marissa Cromer rape file in order to review it. I could see that it was attached to the file relating to the sexual assault on Janice Roberts. The two cases shown as linked crimes by the investigators back in 1992. I was now hoping to not only prove they were linked, but also to prove who was responsible.

The forensic scientists had retained the used condom from the attack on Janice and there was plenty of material to work from. They soon had a full male DNA profile from the semen. The problems with this case would always be to prove what offence the offender had committed as there was still no account from the victim. I made enquiries at St Mathias Lodge and Janice was still a resident there, but the health care officials were adamant that nothing could be achieved by interviewing her and in fact, it would be detrimental to her wellbeing. I considered the possibility of using the attack on Marissa Cromer as similar fact evidence, thus using each offence to provide support for each other.

The DNA profile for the attack on Janice was loaded onto the national DNA database and I received a match against Matthew Anthony Bailey (14/10/67). The match probability was reported as 1:1 billion meaning the likelihood of someone else being responsible was a billion to one.

Matthew Bailey

As the research to trace Bailey was going on, the forensic scientists located the high vaginal swabs taken from Marissa following her rape. These also provided the evidence of a full male profile from semen, and it too was matched to Matthew Bailey. The match probability was again recorded as 1:1 billion. The hunch was right, it was the same offender for both cases, and I now had the name of the man.

I am always interested to know the type of offence committed by an offender, that resulted in them being swabbed and their profile ending up on the National DNA database. I worked closely with the force training officer to produce a training package encouraging new officers to take DNA swabs from offenders whenever the law allowed it. With more offenders' DNA profiles held on the database there is a greater chance of obtaining matches with crime scene DNA.

So why was Matthew Bailey's DNA on the DNA database? In 2003, Constable Scott Westbrook-Smith was a young uniform Police Constable working in the Filton area of Bristol. He attended an anonymous report of an untaxed car parked by the roadside. Scott noticed that the car was in fact displaying a tax disc, but it was for another vehicle. Scott made enquiries and established that the tax disc had been reported as stolen a few streets away. The registered owner of the untaxed car was Matthew Bailey, and he was arrested on suspicion of the theft of the car tax. He admitted to finding the tax disc in the street and keeping it to use on his own car. Matthew Bailey was cautioned for offences of handling stolen goods and fraudulently displaying the car tax. What was most important was that Scott obtained Bailey's fingerprints and DNA sample for loading on the national databases. Had he not done this, Bailey may never have been identified as responsible for the attacks on Janice and Marissa.

Bailey was arrested on 31st March 2004 but when he was interviewed at Southmead police station by DC Pete James and I, regarding both offences, he responded 'no comment' to all questions asked. He was not going to make things easy. An evidential DNA sample was obtained from Bailey as this would need to be compared against both crime scene profiles in order that the evidence could be put before the courts. Bailey was released on bail to await the final forensic results. Forensic tests confirmed the matches to Bailey with a statistical figure of 1 in a billion for both attacks. Once Bailey surrendered to his bail, he was charged with both sexual assaults. He tried to put on a smile, but it was obvious he knew that he would get a lengthy sentence.

On 25th October 2004 at Bristol Crown Court, Matthew Bailey pleaded guilty to the rape of Marissa Cromer and guilty to GBH and indecent assault on Janice Roberts. He was sentenced to life imprisonment.

Marissa made the brave decision to speak with a journalist and to give an interview regarding her experiences at the time of her rape, the service provided by the police, and how she was dealt with by police from the cold case team many years on. The interview was featured in two prominent women's magazines and aimed at encouraging women to report offences of rape and support cold case investigations.

Two more very brave victims that eventually got the justice they deserved due to the hard work of the cold case team.

The Railway Attacker

Chapter 1:

Vanessa – June 1980

Vanessa North was aged just 21 years old and she lived in shared accommodation in the Redland area of Bristol. It was about midnight on 30th June 1980 and it was abnormally warm. Vanessa was walking in Meridian Road, Bristol heading home. She was wearing a floral knee length dress and a white jacket. She noticed a dark coloured car parked at the junction with Archfield Road and a man aged in his late 20's getting out of the driver's side. She thought nothing of it and carried on walking towards Redland Grove. The man approached her from behind and immediately placed his left hand over her mouth and held a sharp knife to her throat. He was quietly spoken when he instructed her not to scream threatening to 'Stick the knife in her' if she failed to obey his instructions. He told her he would do her no harm provided she did exactly what she was told.

He still held the knife to her throat as he walked her across Redland Grove to a grassy area behind the Redland railway station. He took her along the fence by the railway line to a tree in the corner of the field. He had clearly planned this location all along, it was pitch black and very silent. He told her to remove her jacket and to place her hands on the fence in front of her, facing away from him. Whilst stood behind her, he fondled her breasts over her clothing and complimented her on the firmness of her breasts. He then instructed Vanessa to lie on her back and to remain silent. He knelt beside her and reached up under her skirt then started to tug at her knickers, she could hear the material rip as he used his knife to cut at her knickers and remove the gusset exposing the flesh beneath. He initially inserted his finger inside her but she was soon aware of the cold metallic feel of the knife being slowly inserted into her and moving within. She was petrified that she would be disfigured for life or even worse, killed. She had no idea what his intention was but he appeared to be enjoying holding this power over her. She felt him release his grip on the knife and left it protruding from her body as he reached into his pocket and took out a pair of very dark sunglasses. Vanessa was told to wear the sunglasses, and without saying a word, she put them on. If he was hoping the glasses would prevent her from seeing his face it was already too late. She had an image of him burnt into her memory already. He was white, tall and skinny with long dark hair and moustache.

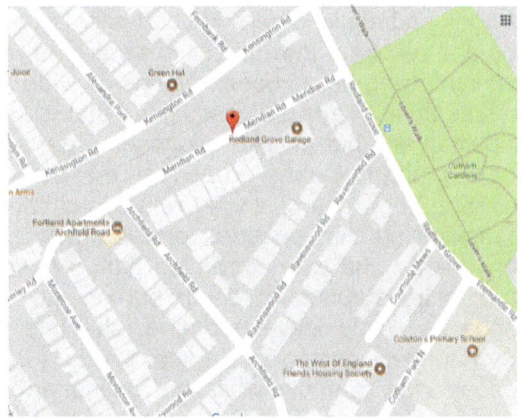

Scene of Vanessa's attack

Vanessa could then feel the knife being slowly and carefully removed from her, she felt the point of the blade as it scratched her insides, she had no pain of being cut which was a relief, but she did feel the trickle of blood as the knife eventually left her body. Her attacker then took out a small torch from his pocket and switched it on. The torch gave out a thin ray of bright white light. Her attacker reached down and parted Vanessa's legs and shone the torch to look inside her and explore her intimately, he penetrated her with the torch and moved it about inside her. This behaviour had by now aroused the attacker sufficiently that he inserted his erect penis inside her continuing with his abuse of her body by ejaculating within her. Vanessa was then made to lie face down whilst her attacker continued his assault. He parted her buttocks and shone the torch, lighting up her anus and inserted the torch inside her, moving it around once again; he continued by digitally penetrating her body and abusing her. He began to lick her anus and reached down to lick her between her legs, instructing her to open her legs as wide as she was able. Vanessa complained that it was too painful and her attacker stopped. He made her sit up and forced her to perform oral sex on him. She knew she could not refuse and could not risk biting him so she complied with his every wish. She was convinced that she was going to be stabbed to death but on the off chance he would leave her alive, she had to obey his every demand. He kept insisting that she look away from him whilst he continued with his vicious attack. The attacker stopped as quickly as he had started and once the ordeal was over, he sat alongside Vanessa on the ground and asked her if she was a virgin or whether she did similar things with her boyfriend. He enquired if she was on the pill and Vanessa told him that she was. The attacker then raped her one final time successfully ejaculating once more. He got dressed and emptied Vanessa's handbag onto the floor and sorted through the contents stealing a £5 note. He read out her name and address that he had found on her driving licence and told her that he now knew where she lived, so he could hurt her at any time he wished. He told her to count slowly to one hundred before getting dressed. At that moment, he collected his sunglasses from her face and walked away. Vanessa was so traumatised that she did exactly as she had been told and only started to get dressed after counting to one hundred. Vanessa had to walk all the way home where she was met by her flat mate and burst into tears.

The police arrived about 15 minutes later and Vanessa took them to the location where the rape had taken place. She was then taken to Redland Police station and asked to wait in a small doctor's surgery, located within the cell block at the station. There was a further delay of 30 minutes before the police surgeon arrived to examine her. She had some swelling and bruising to her labia, a small cut inside her, no doubt from the knife, but no other injuries. Intimate samples were gathered by the doctor who took swabs from her anus, vagina, mouth and face. Vanessa's clothing was seized and placed in individual bags, labelled and sealed to retain any evidence that the attacker had left behind. Vanessa was very tired by this stage, so arrangements were made for her to make a statement later that day and a photofit the following day.

Photofit prepared by Vanessa

It was from the high vaginal swabs that the forensic scientists discovered semen present. This, once again, could only be tested using the blood grouping available to the scientists in 1980 and they could provide evidence that the attacker was blood group 'O'. The blood grouping would never identify the offender but would assist the police in eliminating any suspects.

A major incident room was set up and the investigation lasted for eight months before the disappointing decision had to be made for the case to be filed as undetected.

Vanessa was left to rebuild her life and learn to deal with the demons in her mind.

Chapter 2:

Thomas Stewart – March 2004

In March 2004, I commenced my review into the rape of Vanessa North. The horrendous nature of the attack was obviously apparent and made this a case that I was desperate to solve. Enquiries were made with the Forensic Science Service and the forensic scientist Andrew Parry was allocated the case for further forensic testing. The high vaginal swab and slide, Exhibit IRP6 were located and there was still semen present. Andrew decided that LCN (Low Copy Number) DNA testing was the best process to use on the sample and within a month he was able to report that the vaginal swab had given up mixed DNA profiles. The result indicated the presence of DNA from a male as well as DNA of a female. This was to be expected as this type of DNA testing was much more sensitive and the finding of both the partial DNA profiles was very encouraging as it was likely a mix of the victim's profile and the male offender. In order to obtain a more detailed result, Andrew stated further work could be done to improve the result.

By November 2004, the further work had been completed and improved the male profile, but Andrew needed a DNA reference sample from Vanessa to assist with analysis and interpretation of the results.

Major Crime Investigation Officer Phil Lewis was tasked with locating Vanessa in order to obtain a voluntary DNA swab from her. She was traced to Scotland, and this would be the first time she had been spoken to about the attack on her since the case was filed in 1981. It came as a great shock to her that her attack was still being investigated but she was very keen to assist the investigation in any way possible.

I had by now been the Cold Case supervisor for nearly two years instead of the planned six months and was due to hand over the cold case work to Detective Sergeant Mike Britton. I had constantly delayed my departure in a hope that the forensic results would arrive and lead to the offender being identified in the Vanessa North case and another case I had started to review. At this time, I only had a partial male profile which was being improved upon but fell short of a full profile necessary to identify a suspect. Andrew Parry could give me no indication as to how long it would take for the full results to be available. I reluctantly handed over the reins to Mike Britton knowing that he would do an excellent job in my place. He wasn't initially keen on doing cold case work but very soon got hooked.

By March 2005, the forensic results had not come through and, although tantalisingly close, I had by then returned to live Major Crime duties and Mike Britton was in charge of cold cases. It was only one month later, on 11th April 2005 that there was a reported DNA match on the enhanced partial profile from the Vanessa

North rape. The suspect was identified as Thomas Ian Stewart born in1950. The statistic for the match was 1: 360,000 and not the 1: Billion that is normally hoped for with a full profile.

This was very strong evidence and the fact that Stewart was a Bristol criminal who fit the general description given by Vanessa in 1980 was very good. Stewart was a convicted murderer and out on life licence.

Andrew Parry continued to carry out more forensic tests in a hope of improving the statistical match result by obtaining a fuller profile. The further forensic work was slow and meticulous, but improvements were made. By August 2005, the statistical match had improved to 1: 85 million.

On 17th August 2005, Thomas Stewart was arrested for the rape of Vanessa North. He denied the offence claiming to have no knowledge of the incident whatsoever. The strength of the evidence was sufficient for the CPS to agree that he should be charged and remanded in custody.

Thomas Stewart

Prior to the trial, the forensic evidence was worked on further by Andrew and by September 2005 the DNA match statistic had reached 1:340 million.

The trial was held at Bristol Crown Court on 13th November 2006 and lasted 4 days, the jury found Stewart guilty of rape and he was sentenced to 10 years imprisonment.

Judge Carol Hagan said of Stewart "*The degree of harm you did in terms of psychological damage is immense. I regard the risk you pose as real and continuing.*"

Stewart's murder conviction was of a 36-year-old man, Richard Lyddon in the lavatory at Reading railway station. The motive for that crime was never established but Stewart was under the influence of alcohol at the time. Lyddon was a male nurse from Taunton, and he had travelled to Reading railway station to catch a connecting train to London to attend a job interview. Richard went into the toilet cubicle and Thomas Stewart immediately burst in and pinned Richard to the seat and stabbed him with a 9" bowie style knife. The ticket collector heard the commotion and entered the toilets to investigate. Stewart convinced the rail employee that nothing was wrong and as soon the man left Stewart stabbed Lyddon two more times before casually walking out. Lyddon managed to stagger out onto the platform but died soon afterwards. This just demonstrates the type of callous individual Thomas Stewart was.

The next case that I want to write about was the last case I reviewed before passing all the cold cases over to Mike Britton. It was the second case that I referred to earlier that caused me to delay my departure because I really wanted to see it through to its conclusion. The fact that the case involved an elderly victim that was attacked in bed at home, made it even more horrendous. The victim was now deceased and this made me even more determined to get justice for her.

Monstrous Case of Rape

Chapter 1:

Valerie – April 1983

Valerie Neil was a very independent woman, she had been living on her own for a long time, since her husband died in 1963. She had no family living locally and she didn't want to go into a nursing home, even when she became frail in her old age. At the time of the attack, she was 82 years old and lived in her semi-detached Victorian style house in the St Andrews area of Bristol. Valerie hardly ever left the house due to her fragility, but she could get about indoors and was able to cook and look after herself. The house was in great need of repair, the front door had not shut properly for several months but Valerie hadn't been bothered with finding a handyman as she hardly ever used the door in any case. She loved the area she lived in and liked the fact that the street outside was very quiet.

It was about 2:00am on 26th April 1983 and Valerie was asleep in bed wearing her long thick nightie as she found it a little cold in the house at night. She slept fairly well, normally going to bed about 9:00pm and not getting up until 9:00am. She had no idea what woke her on this particular night but as she opened her eyes, she could see a man stood above her looking down, with his trousers dropped around his ankles, he was masturbating himself. *"What do you want?"* she said in a feisty way *"Get out!"* She started to sit up but the man pushed her back on the bed and held her firmly by pushing down on her chest. She looked to her side and could see her husband's war medals peeping out from beneath the pillows on her bed. She had always slept with the medals since her husband's death many years earlier. She quickly covered them over as there was no way the medals were going to be taken by this man. He pushed a sock in her mouth making her nearly choke and he tied it in position with the cord from her dressing gown. Whilst she was gagging, he tied her hands using one of her stockings that he found in her bedroom drawer and placed a blindfold over her eyes which she believed was one of her old scarves. Valerie could hardly move and was finding it hard to breathe. The attacker then grabbed the top of her nightie and ripped it open fully leaving her lying naked on the bed. He then climbed on top of her and lay between her legs and forced his penis into her and raped her. He was still wearing his upper clothing, but his trousers were somewhere around his ankles or possibly on the floor by this stage. Valerie was later to tell the police that she did not think that he ejaculated but could not be sure. Once the man had satisfied his evil urges, he stopped, got off the bed pulled his trousers up and wiped her between the legs using some sort of material, he was obviously intent on removing any evidence. He placed the cloth in his pocket before starting to search the bedroom cupboards and drawers. He left the room, but she could still hear him rummaging around the rest of the house before she heard the sound of the front door slamming as he left. He stole money and jewellery from the house worth about £15.

Valerie struggled to free her hands and was eventually able to remove the blindfold and gag. The first thing she checked was that her husband's medals were safe under her pillows. She put on some clothing and slowly walked next door to call a neighbour for help.

The police were there in minutes but an area search found no-one. Valerie could not assist with a description of her attacker but was able to provide a ten-page statement detailing her ordeal. She was medically examined and her clothing was seized. The usual intimate swabs were taken and these included combings from her pubic hairs. She found the whole experience very degrading but was insistent that she had to do everything she could to help the police capture her attacker. The police believed that the most likely point of entry to her house was the insecure front door.

The forensic results were very disappointing, with no semen being detected and no offender blood grouping established. The police looked at known burglars and sexual offenders that were linked to the St Andrews area but it was only a matter of months before the case was filed with no offender being identified. Valerie's jewellery never surfaced and although burglary was considered the most likely motive, a sexual predator could not be ruled out. With no forensic evidence or fingerprints to assist with proving the identity of the offender little could be done so the case was filed as undetected.

Chapter 2:

The Davis Brothers – April 2004

It was in April 2004 that I commenced the review of the Valerie Neil rape investigation. Although this was a case where in 1983, it had been reported that no forensic evidence had been found. I could not accept that this was the end of the line for this investigation. I enquired about what exhibits were still retained by the Forensic Science Service in order that I could discuss with them any possible forensic testing that could be considered now. They had very little material left but did still have the pubic hair combings. It was a long shot but as the offender had, at some point, been led on top of Valerie when he raped her, there was a possibility that he could have shed his own pubic hair or even deposited some semen, which could be caught within the combings. It was agreed that the pubic hair combings would be examined for any hairs with suitable root material for DNA profiling or any other foreign material. The exhibit would be tested by using the latest SGM+ DNA technology and if unsuccessful LCN DNA would also be considered. LCN DNA is often referred to as Low Copy Number DNA and is a technique sensitive enough to analyse just a few cells. It takes a small amount of DNA and copies it, so that a larger sample profile can be created for testing. It can help solve cases where there is only a minute amount of DNA left by the perpetrator.

It took up until August 2005 and numerous forensic tests later that a male DNA profile was found from a rooted pubic hair. Mike Britton was running the Cold Case Team by this stage, and he was delighted with the news. He would always keep me updated with developments because he knew the effort that I had put into the case to persistently push for the latest DNA testing. He knew how much the case meant to me as he was now totally committed to it as well. This profile was loaded onto the national DNA database and matched with Mark Anthony Davis born in 1957. The match probability was reported as 1: 43 million. Research into Davis showed him to be a Bristol burglar who had been living in the St Andrews area at the time of the rape. He was a drug abuser and regularly committed thefts or burglaries to feed his drug habit. He was traced to Oxford and arrested on 5th August 2005.

In interview, Davis denied the offence and when asked to account for the DNA match from a hair found in the victim's pubic hair combings, he came up with the following defence.

Mark Davis

The DNA match was not 1: billion match, so he claimed it could have been his brother's hair. He claimed that, like him, his brother was a burglar and had been living with him in St Andrews at the time. He stated that his brother was dead so could not be questioned. This was potentially an issue that would need resolving and Mike and his team had soon confirmed that Mark's brother, Graham had been a burglar and had lived in St Andrews and had died from a drugs overdose in 2000. Graham's DNA profile was not on the DNA database and had never been taken by the police. What the police did have was a set of Graham's fingerprints. Mike had the fantastic idea of using the fingerprint forms, which Graham had obviously touched when giving his finger impressions and to swab the fingerprint forms only on the areas containing prints. It was from this process that a male DNA profile was obtained. By then swabbing other members of the Davis family, Graham's DNA profile could be determined and he could be eliminated as the offender.

Because of the efforts Mike Britton had put into clearing Graham, Mark Davis pleaded guilty at Bristol Crown Court on 26th June 2006 and was sentenced to nine years in prison with an order to be placed on the sex offenders register for life.

When sentencing him, Judge Tom Crowther QC said it was *"One of the most monstrous cases of rape."*

It was established that Mrs Neil had died in 1989 not knowing her attacker would someday be caught. A statement was released by her family who said she never forgot the attack; it had badly affected her and she found it difficult to cope. What her attacker had done was disgusting, to attack a defenceless, elderly woman in her home - she didn't stand a chance.

This was Mike's first cold case conviction, and he was hooked.

Between 2003 and 2008 when I finally retired from the Avon and Somerset police as a police officer, seventeen rapists had been convicted as the result of the Cold Case Teams hard work. It made me very proud that I had set up the unit from nothing and it was being left in a much healthier state than when I had started. I, in fact only had two weeks leave following my retirement before I then commenced employment as a Major Crime Investigations Officer with the Avon and Somerset's Major Crime Review Team. This team was created to review murder and stranger rape offences that were undetected after one month and to assist in identifying new lines of investigation. I was in my element and was pleased to be able to give investigating officers guidance and assistance in detecting stranger rape offences. I hoped to help reduce the numbers of cold cases in the future and to get victims their justice much sooner.

There were still a number of outstanding cold cases that I had worked on prior to my retirement. Some had full offender DNA profiles and were awaiting DNA matches to be reported in the future, some had partial profiles and required further advancements in forensic science to achieve better results. The Avon and Somerset were in a much better position regarding their undetected historic crimes and the cold cases were left to be managed by the forces Major Crime Unit who predominantly deal with live murder investigations.

In 2009, it became apparent that without a dedicated lead for cold case investigations, the results had started to tail off, so it was decided that the management should be transferred to the Major Crime Review Team. This felt like it was my baby coming home and I soon set about the task of refamiliarising myself with the cases and getting up to date with any progress that had been made since I had last worked them. I started identifying new offences that would need to be reviewed. I also needed to get myself fully briefed on the current forensic techniques available for testing exhibits. With the assistance of Cellmark a forensic provider to the police, I spent many hours with them discussing cases and deciding what matters should be prioritised.

Detective Sergeant Julie Mackay joined the review team later in 2009 and she was to supervise me and the rest of the small team. Julie was a vivacious, enthusiastic 38-year-old and I knew I could work well with her as she had been one of my young trainee detectives when I was a detective sergeant at Staplehill police station. Julie always made herself approachable and made you feel free to openly discuss your views and worries about any cases. She had some very strong characters to deal with in the unit, experienced ex detective sergeants like myself and Alan Andrews. It was strange in the mixed gender office to be often heard discussing semen, intimate parts of the male or female anatomy and the ability of men to ejaculate for a second time soon after the first. I have no idea what outsiders must have thought when they walked in on one of these discussions. I became the office expert on all things DNA and my knowledge was all picked up from talking with the many forensic scientists I worked with over the years.

All the cold cases I have written about so far were reasonably straight forward because as soon as the scientists obtained the full offender DNA profile, it matched to someone already on the national DNA database. It was then a matter of tracing the suspect and recreating a prosecution file in order to get the case through the courts. The next two cases I am now going to write about were much more complex.

The Baptist Chapel Rape

Chapter 1:

Samantha – January 1986

Samantha was only 20 years old and she had lived quite a hard life, she left home at 17 and had been sleeping in various squats with several friends ever since. She was a drug addict and an alcoholic and had suffered from various mental health issues. She was a pretty young woman 5'4" tall and slim build with long wild mousey brown hair. She had spent the evening in a friend's squat smoking cannabis and consuming vodka. She was quite merry but not in her mind drunk. As was normal for her, she had no money left and no transport to get home so she would walk from St Pauls to her home in Southville, Bristol where her current squat was located. The walk would take her about 40 minutes, but she had no choice.

It was the early hours of the 30th of January 1986 so it was cold and windy but fortunately it was not raining. She was wrapped up warm, dressed in trousers, a jumper and overcoat. Samantha set off at about midnight and walked steadily through the streets that she knew well; she had spent many an afternoon selling the 'Big Issue' or begging for money and considered herself as being very street wise. She knew two or three of the other squatters would be at home to greet her and they would all sit together to have another smoke and drink before going to bed. Samantha had got as far as the bottom of Stokes Croft, intending to cross over by the bear pit, past the coach station and head towards the city centre. She saw the man stood on the corner smoking. He was a black male, quite stocky build and aged in his mid-thirties. He shouted out to her from a distance *"Hi gorgeous, do you want company?"* She declined the offer by ignoring him and continued walking, but within a minute or so he was walking alongside her, trying to chat her up. He gave her his name and asked if she fancied going out with him, but she was used to men trying to chat her up, she was not worried but so as not to offend him she spoke politely back and made small talk. The man followed her all the way through the city centre and into Bedminster as far as East Street, constantly pestering her for a date. She didn't want to annoy him but also didn't want to lead him on so she told him that she was almost home and invented the fact that her boyfriend would be waiting up for her to arrive. She was in fact still some distance from her squat in Southville but decided to turn left into Phillip Street because she did not want this man knowing where she lived.

At that moment, the man's attitude changed, and he punched Samantha in the side of the head, knocking her to the ground. He dragged her 30 metres into a nearby church doorway and forced her to lie down on her back. With one hand over her mouth and the other pressing down on her shoulders, he told her if she screamed, he would strangle her. The man was too strong for her, and she was not able to scream even if she had wanted to as the fear going through her body made her freeze. The man slowly removed his right hand from her mouth, making it clear what he would do if she shouted out. He reached down fumbling at her trousers and slowly pulled the zip down. His grubby hand then moved into the gap that the open zip left, he pulled her knickers to one side and with his fingers he started to touch her and enter her body. Samantha just laid there absolutely still hoping he would stop. He then undid the button of her trousers and aggressively pulled them down, removing them, leaving them on the ground by her feet. He grabbed at her knickers and viciously yanked at them making them rip slightly but staying in place. Samantha made a conscious decision to fight back at this stage, she was determined not to let this man rape her. As she fought back, her bracelet snapped and fell in pieces on the floor to the side of where she lay. She felt another heavy blow to the head. She was semi-conscious and helpless and had to accept the inevitable as he ripped away her knickers and threw them down to join her trousers on the floor. He was already erect and penetrated her forcibly, causing her excruciating pain, she could feel as he almost immediately ejaculated inside her. The rape was over in seconds and the man rolled to one side in a state of relaxation. Samantha took the chance to push him off and jump up. She grabbed her clothing, turned and ran straight down the main road to a nearby printing firm that was open for business. She burst into tears as she explained to the foreman what had happened to her, and he checked outside to confirm that her attacker was gone. The foreman called the police, and it was not long before a policewoman was there recording the details of the crime. Samantha had a medical examination that same morning, she provided the doctor with all the usual intimate medical samples and handed over her clothes to the officer. The police had to provide her with a change of clothes as she had no others to wear at her squat.

The following morning the case was allocated to DC Frank Spiller to deal with, believe it or not I was the Acting Detective Sergeant allocated to supervise the case. I was a 28-year-old detective, who had joined the police aged 18, I had become a detective in 1983 and had been based in Bishopsworth Bristol for all my CID life. I was keen, enthusiastic and I think popular with all my colleagues because I was a hard grafter. It was due to my tenacious attitude to work that I had been asked to supervise others.

Samantha's medical examination showed that she had sustained some minor scratches and bruising. The church doorway where the attack had happened was located with Samantha's help, her broken bracelet still laid in pieces on the floor. The scene was later examined and photographed by the scenes of crime officer.

It had been my decision which seized exhibits from the victim should be submitted to the lab. I decided that Samantha's trousers and knickers should be sent, as well as her intimate swabs. These were the most likely items that would detect the presence of semen and a later submission of her upper clothing could follow if early results failed to find anything.

It was the vaginal swabs that gave the positive result that we were hoping for, the semen on them was able to provide the blood group of the offender. This was unfortunately a blood group that thirty per cent of the male population had, so supported the fact that Samantha had been sexually assaulted but provided limited evidence to identify an offender. The forensic results would however assist in eliminating some suspects as they were identified.

Two local residents were arrested on description, but they were both eliminated on blood grouping.

The investigation to trace the offender had begun but after six months of enquiries and no offender being identified, Frank filed the papers as an undetected cold case. The system for filing crimes at Bishopsworth police station resulted in the papers being stored in a locked cupboard, where file after file were added over the years and regular weeding of stored material was carried out. This was to prove problematical in the future.

This file was missing when I was searching for all the undetected cold case rape offences back in 2003. The crime was on my spreadsheet, but the sheet had to be endorsed 'Missing File'. It was believed that the papers had either been mistakenly thrown out and shredded during one of the periodic weeding procedures or they had been amongst stored crime reports in the Bridewell police cells when they flooded. In any case nothing was left to review.

I actually had no recollection in 2003 that I had played some role in the investigation, and it was simply just another unfortunate missing file that we could not review without paperwork.

Chapter 2:

Valentine Barnett – September 2010

The Forensic Science Service was given funds by the government as part of Operation Stealth, and scientists decided that the best use of the money was for them to do their own review of material they held in storage. They assessed all their stored exhibits and made their own decision as to which were worthy of further forensic testing. They planned to contact the police forces in question only after they had concluded the additional forensic testing and could assist in identifying an offender.

Unbeknown to the Avon and Somerset police, the laboratory located Samantha's high vaginal swabs and examined them using DNA technology. They were able to obtain a 19-allele, male profile from the semen. A full DNA profile at this time was 20 alleles so this was an almost complete profile. When they loaded this onto the National DNA database, there was no match against any individual on the database. They were however able to report that the DNA profile matched another undetected crime scene stain. This other crime was a burglary in 41, Croft Road, St Pauls, Bristol and had occurred on 27th August 2003.

Julie Mackay our supervisor was sent the information regarding the DNA scene to scene match and allocated it to me to investigate, although at that stage neither she nor I, knew that I had some previous dealings with the case. We had no paperwork for the rape due to the missing file and we had never previously made enquiries to locate any undetected burglary files. In fact, the files for undetected burglaries were regularly weeded from the system so there was a possibility that it also may never be found. Knowing how submissions to the forensic laboratory were made, I contacted the lab to see what additional information they held. The police would often submit copies of victim statements and crime reports to help scientists understand the case better when interpreting results. The Forensic Science Service was only able to supply copies of the original police submission paperwork and when that arrived, I was surprised and amused to see it, as I immediately recognised my own handwriting all over it. I could not remember this specific case as 20 years of dealing with assorted crimes prevented me from recalling them all. I realised that I had been involved with the rape of Samantha even if it was only as a supervisor so I knew that I should find something in my old pocketbooks and diaries.

NOTE: 1. Each article submitted must be properly packed and labelled.
2. The description and identification mark given below must correspond exactly with that on the label.
3. Continue on separate sheet if necessary but in sequence as below.

Serial Number	Identifying Mark	Description of Article(s)	From whom and where taken	Place, date and time found and by whom.
RJV1	1 pair jeans trousers		Taken from complainant
RJV2	Ladies pants		at 4.45 am 30.1.86 at Broadway Road P.1. by WR Vickery
RJV4	1 pair disposable pants		As above at 6.30 am 30.1.86 by WR Vickery
SFD1	Control Swab		
SFD2	External vaginal swab		Taken by Dr D.I.Dixon at surgery at Broadway Road Police Station 4.45 30.1.96
SFD3	Low Internal vaginal swab		
SFD4	High Internal vaginal swab		
SFD5	Pubic hair swab		
SFD6	Cut pubic hair		
SF07	Combed Pubic hair		
SSD10	Blood Sample		
SSD11	Saliva Sample.		

(13) (a) What is required to be established or proved in relation to items submitted (b) Quote Laboratory Reference number of previous submissions
(c) Show brief details of proposed charges

Examine for traces or presence of semen. If any found could it be grouped to be compared with any future samples from suspects.

(14) Signature and rank of Supervisory Officer authorising submission .... CDT Morris .... A.S.O.

(15) Method of delivery of articles to laboratory—*By Hand, Registered Post or Recorded Delivery.

Person delivering articles	Name (Block letters)	Rank ....
	Signature	Date ....
Received at the laboratory by	Name (Block letters) .... RODNICK	Rank OV
	Signature	Date 12170

(16) Method of return of articles—*By Hand, Registered Post or Recorded Delivery.

| Person receiving articles | Name (Block letters) .... | Rank .... |
| | Signature .... Hayes | Date .... |

(17) Person returning articles | Name (Block letters) .... | Rank .... |
| | Signature .... Coburn | Date .... |

*Delete as necessary

Page 2 of the forensic submission form bearing my signature

The forensic submission form alone provided the details of the case officer, DC Frank Spiller. I knew that Frank had died as I had attended the funeral only three years earlier. The names of a female Police chaperone, WPC Vickery who had seized Samantha's clothing and the Doctor who examined Samantha were recorded on the form and I set about tracking them down.

Dr Dibden had been a regular police surgeon who was often called out to examine rape victims. She was now retired but still lived in north Bristol. I phoned her up, explained the situation and Dr Dibden was able to confirm she had maintained a hardback book of details of all her old police examinations, and she knew exactly where it was in her attic as she had only looked at it a few days earlier when clearing out the loft, she had considered throwing it away but fortunately for me she hadn't. Dr Dibden had kept meticulous notes, even an accurate account given by the victim about exactly what had happened. The notes also gave details of the nights Detective Constable, Bob Wallington who was the first detective officer to attend the scene. Dr Dibden supplied a lengthy statement and the re-building of the investigation file had started. Although we had no copy of the victim's original statement, we did now have her account of the attack. I did not wish to contact the victim at this stage as we still had no idea who the offender was so didn't want to raise her expectation of a prosecution only to fail in ever finding the culprit.

I now had to continue with my rebuilding of the rape investigation to see if there were any suspects I could now swab to eliminate or prove they were responsible for the rape.

WPC Vickery had retired and re-married but I traced her to an address in Somerset. She had no recollection of the offence but using the details recorded on the forensic submission form, she was able to supply a statement. Her pocketbook for 1986 was never found.

I knew Bob Wallington quite well; we had been detectives together in Bishopsworth CID office and he was another colleague that I was supervising at the time of the rape. I knew that Bob had retired as a police officer but like myself, had returned to work for the police as a civilian employee. Bob still had all his old CID diaries and had detailed entries about his attendance at Philip Street. It was while questioning Bob and obtaining his statement that I learnt about Samantha's bracelet having been broken and found at the crime scene. Bob was also able to give me the names of two employees at the printing firm that Samantha had run to and the name of the Scenes of Crime officer who had attended the scene.

It was quite a challenge to trace the foreman of the printing company because the company had twice been bought out over the years. I traced a company director from a printing business in Portbury, Bristol who used to work for the Philip Street printers and knew that the foreman involved lived in the Chew Magna area. With a name and area of where he lived, I was soon on the heels of the foreman and met him at his Chew Magna address for a statement. He had no trouble recollecting the incident as he explained that it is not every day you are confronted by a terrified woman alleging rape. He was able to provide important evidence of early complaint and Samantha's state immediately after the attack.

I checked my own historic CID diaries and could see that I had, in fact, met Samantha in 1986 to show her a series of photographs of potential suspects and that she had failed to identify her attacker.

Knowing that the scene of crime officer had attended, I assumed that he would have taken photographs of the scene. The lab submission form indicated that the scene was a church doorway and Bob had spoken about a broken necklace. I paid a visit to the police HQ photographic department who told me that all photographic negatives taken from crime scenes were stored in a warehouse in Clevedon. The negatives were stored in crates by year so I would need to look for 1986 negatives for Bristol offences. I located three cardboard boxes full of old black and white crime scene photographic negatives at the storage facility. The only way to go through these was to hold up each one at a time to the light to discover the images they held. There were hundreds of post-mortem photographs, crime scenes images and injury photographs but nothing to indicate where the negatives I wanted were. There was no short cut, I would simply have to look at them all and even then, hope I would recognise them if I saw them. I was halfway through the third box, and beginning to think my luck was out when I picked out two images that stood out. There was an arched doorway on one and a broken bead bracelet on the second. Had I found the scene photographs. I got the negatives developed so I now had black and white photographs in my possession.

1986 photographs of the chapel and bracelet

I knew where the crime scene was, so I went to the scene with the photographs and was satisfied that I now had the original scene photographs. The scene had changed to some degree so I requested a new set of coloured photographs to be taken that I could use for court if I ever identified the offender.

The original Scene of Crime Officer, Bob Harding was still employed in the police, and he came out to take the new colour images. He then provided a statement of his visits to the scene in 1986 and 2010.

2010 photograph of crime scene

The file was slowly coming together but the two most important things were missing. A full account from Samantha would be required. She had made a statement in 1986 but this was missing, so an account would need to be captured again, this I decided would be delayed until after the second most important matter was dealt with. The offender had to be identified.

The only line of enquiry that had not been investigated was the burglary that had a DNA match to the same offender as the rape.

Fortunately, I located a copy of the original burglary crime report at Trinity Road crime storage facilities and from this, I began to learn more about that crime.

At about 4am on 27th August 2003, Mrs Janice Peters was at home alone at 41 Croft Road, St Pauls, Bristol. She was disturbed by a noise coming from one of the other upstairs rooms. She got up to investigate. As she entered her bathroom, she noticed that the bathroom window was open and was sure that she had closed it prior to going to bed. Mrs Peters also noticed a line of blood on the side of the bath panel, which again, she was convinced had not been there before. When she looked out of the window, she saw 4 black males running across the rear gardens. Her house was a terraced two up two down style property. Mrs Peters checked and could find nothing stolen but, due to the shock the incident had caused her, she phoned the police. Not only were the crime details recorded but a Scenes of Crime officer attended the address and swabbed the blood from the bath panel and submitted it to the Forensic Science Service for DNA examination.

A full male profile was obtained and loaded onto the National DNA database, and it was this profile that later matched to the Samantha rape profile.

It was recorded by the CSI on the rear of the crime report 'I have tested blood found on bath and it is human. The occupants of the address have all stated it was not theirs'.

I felt that as nothing had been stolen in the burglary and that there was a reference to other occupants living at the address, it was worth contacting Mrs Peters. I explained to Janice that I was investigating her burglary from 2003 and was aware about the blood that was discovered on the bath panel. I informed her that a male DNA profile from that blood was still on the national DNA database and from reading the file, I wanted to establish if any other male occupants had lived or stayed at the house at the time of the burglary. I felt it could have been that the blood on the bath came from another occupant of the house rather than come from a burglar. Janice said she doubted it very much, but she accepted it was possible. I told her I needed to eliminate any other male occupant of the house as we did not wish DNA on the database unless it was the burglar's. She stated that the only male at the house was her partner Valentine Barnett and she offered to pass the phone over to Valentine so I could speak directly to him. Valentine could not recall ever having dripped blood onto the bath panel but accepted it was possible. He agreed to provide a voluntary DNA swab for elimination once I had explained that the voluntary swab would only be checked directly against the burglary profile and not compared against any other crimes.

I knew of course that if the voluntary swab from Mr Barnett did match the blood on the bath, it would indirectly be matching the rape profile and would provide the intelligence to justify Valentine's arrest for rape.

I attended Croft Road the next day by appointment and took a voluntary swab from Mr Barnett. He was a black male born in 1950 so was of the right ethnicity and age to have been Samantha's attacker. The swab was sent to the Forensic Science Service, and I knew that I would have a long wait for the result. Patience was not one of my strong points.

When the result came that Valentine Barnett's DNA matched the blood on the bath, I was both shocked and excited. I had to make sure that the FSS did not carry out any comparison of Valentine Barnett's DNA with the DNA recovered from Samantha's rape. He had been told his sample would only be checked against the blood at Croft Road and that had to be the case. The fact that we now had intelligence to link him to Samantha's rape would need to be handled very carefully.

I had discussions with Julie about these new developments and you could feel the buzz in the office. When you think about it, luck was again on our side. Had the Scene of Crime Officer taken Valentine's elimination DNA at the time of the burglary, the blood on the bath would have been eliminated and the profile never loaded onto the crime scene profile database. We would never have had a match.

A plan was put in place to trace Samantha, to update her and also to obtain her account of the rape. We also planned for the arrest of Valentine Barnett. Julie coordinated this stage as she knew she would be needed to discuss charging decisions with the CPS after Barnett was interviewed.

Samantha was very pleased with the news and agreed to be video interviewed to record her account of the attack. Video interviewing was not something used back in 1986 but was a much better means of interviewing victims in rape cases. She had no problems remembering even fine details of the assault as she had lived with it daily and was still getting the occasional flash back. One of the most amazing facts that came out of the interview was when Samantha spoke about her attacker having introduced himself. She could recall that he told her his name was Valentine, she had not believed him because Valentine's Day was only 2 weeks away and she thought it was just a chat up line but what a fantastic piece of evidence this was. When he introduced himself to her, Valentine obviously had no plan to rape her, but that idea had developed during the walk to Philip Street.

On 13th September 2010, Julie arrested Valentine Barnett from his home address in Croft Road, unfortunately as a Major Crime Support Officer I no longer had the power to arrest people. I was present and could feel the tension in the air as he was taken away. He was arrested on suspicion of the rape of Samantha in 1986. He made no comment when arrested. I was still able to conduct interviews and can remember sitting opposite him in Trinity Road police station when he attempted to avoid getting charged. He denied ever having sexual intercourse with anyone that he was not in a relationship with. When the details of the offence were explained to him, he denied ever having sexual intercourse outdoors. He also denied having sexual intercourse with anyone without their consent. An evidential DNA swab had to be taken, that could be sent to the lab for direct comparison with the rape profile obtained from the rape of Samantha. Barnett was bailed to return to the police for further questioning after the forensic results would be back.

The forensic evidence confirmed that Barnett was the man who had sex with Samantha on 30th January 1986 and when he answered bail, he was given one further chance to explain himself.

On this occasion when I interviewed Barnett, he decided to change his defence and claimed that in 1986 he was an alcoholic and would often have blackouts. He disputed ever having raped anyone and that, if he had met Samantha, the sex would have been consensual even if it was outdoors. He had to accept that he could not dispute her account of the attack if he was claiming he had no recollection of the encounter due to his blackouts.

Julie spoke with the CPS about the case and they took a lot of persuasion to agree with charging him. The topic of how he was 'duped' into providing his original voluntary swab was discussed but stated cases supported the practice used by the police. The CPS wanted corroboration and the fact that the attacker gave the name Valentine, and the suspect was called Valentine did not seem enough. CPS claimed that it was just a coincidence because it was close to 14th February. The fact that the offender was a black male and offence took place in Bristol and our suspect with matching DNA was a black male from Bristol did not impress them either. Luckily Julie stood her ground, she could be very persuasive when she needed to. The CPS eventually agreed Barnett should be charged.

Barnett as he looked in 1986

Valentine Barnett was charged on 11th January 2011 and bailed to attend Bristol Magistrates court on Valentine's Day 14th February 2011. On his next appearance at Bristol Crown court on 28th February 2011 he pleaded guilty to rape. The judge gave him credit for an early plea and avoiding the cost of a trial. Barnett was sentenced to 7 ½ years in prison.

The effect the rape had on Samantha is best given in her own words:

"The reality of the situation was when I was younger, I had dreams and ambitions to do that cliché thing to marry someone like my Dad and go on to have children. I look back now and realise that the rape meant that I was unable to fulfil any of those ambitions and that the rape took me down a path in life that I never wanted to go down. I saw myself as an adult in a strong relationship with a man and having children – and I am jealous of those people that have that in their lives. In fact, there are times like Christmas when I feel excluded and lonely. I am so angry and very sad about it; I am not the person that I was and the person that I thought I would be."

Julie and I posing for the press following Barnett's conviction

The next case saw Julie and I working together again on Avon and Somerset's largest and most complex cold case ever. We were both still working in the Major Crime Review Team, with Julie supervising six members of staff. The time had come when the cold case murder investigations were due for review. There were twenty-three undetected murder enquiries dating back to 1947. The offences were divided up between the team. I was allocated the 1979 murder of Wendy Jenkins, a prostitute whose body was found on a pile of sand at Backfields, St Pauls, the 1984 murder of Mark Yendall whose body was recovered from the city docks, the 1989 murder of George Thorley who was a homeless man that was beaten to death and sexually assaulted, the 2001 murder of 18 year old Christopher Hewitt, stabbed in the street in Easton Bristol probably over a drugs related dispute. We all carried out a forensic review of the murders allocated to us and reported back to the team to decide which case should take priority.

The 1984 Melanie Road murder was identified as the priority murder to concentrate on as a team. Like all the murders, it had been periodically reviewed and substantial additional forensic work carried out over the years. We now wanted to look afresh at the case.

Murder investigations unlike rape offences are much harder to detail accurately when writing a story. There is no account from the victim about what occurred, rarely any independent witness and the offender often exercises his/her right to remain silent, so their account is not known. It is for that reason that I want to make it clear that this next case is based on my thoughts on what possibly happened. My thoughts are based on all the evidence I read during the review process. I have visited the crime scene and surrounding area several times and I have interviewed many of those people involved in the investigation. Melanie Road as you will read later was stabbed to death in a frenzied attack and was sexually assaulted. The offender when arrested and interviewed has never given an account but has pleaded guilty. Many people have asked if this was his first and only attack, if it is possible that he committed such a violent crime on the one and only occasion he came to the notice of the police. Well, it is possible, but I will leave you to decide if that is likely, once you have read the circumstances. I can say that there is not sufficient evidence that this man has committed other crimes, but I intend to give my personal slant on what may have happened.

Operation Rhodium

Chapter 1:

Melanie – June 1984

The Road family had moved to Bath two years prior when Melanie was 15 years old, she had been going to Bath High School for girls' since moving to Bath and had spent the last month studying for her exams which were due to start the following week. Melanie was quiet, studious and was very hopeful of getting the A levels she required to go to university. She had already made her plans for after university, it would be to travel the world before starting any employment and then who knows. The previous day she had spent some time with her sister and 6-month-old niece. She had given her niece a bath and then held her in her arms whilst giving her a feed. One day she was hoping to have a loving husband and two, may be three children of her own. She was going to live in Bath because she found it a lovely city with nice friendly people and it made her feel safe. Her future was all mapped out but for now she needed to concentrate on studying.

It was a sunny Friday afternoon in June 1984 and 17-year-old Melanie Road was thinking about her school exams. It was too late now but she was confident she had done enough work and would be able to go to university next year.

She was in a happy mood and decided to take a few hours out from her studies to pop into Bath to buy her mum a bunch of flowers for putting up with her mood swings due to the pressures of studying. In order to burn off her excess energy, she had decided to have a few games of tennis with her best friend.

Life was great, Melanie had a boyfriend Sebastian Charalambous who was a Greek national and they had both spoken about spending the summer holidays together in Greece. She was so excited about the idea of spending time together abroad that she was learning to speak Greek and could often be heard saying the odd word such as 'Kalimera' and 'Kalispera'.

Melanie met up with Sebastian and his brother Theo who had unexpectedly arrived from London. They walked to a nearby restaurant for a bite to eat before Melanie returned home and got dressed up to go out to the Beau Nash club in Bath. She had planned to meet up again with her boyfriend, Theo and a friend Denis Costas to spend the evening together. Melanie was wearing a blue blouse, black cardigan, blue ankle length trousers and a pair of cream shoes. She looked smart yet casual as she left home, having written a note to her mother Jean to let her know she would be in late and not to wait up. Melanie walked into the centre of Bath as she had done many times before, it was only half an hour walk from home and she enjoyed taking in the warm summer breeze.

She met up with Sebastian, Theo and Denis and headed off to Beau Nash's Club in Kingston Road, arriving around 11:25pm. They enjoyed their evening dancing to the music of the time such as Chameleon by Boy George. Melanie wasn't drinking much, in fact she only had one glass of wine all evening. The group stayed together and left the club just as it was shutting shortly after 1:30am on the Saturday morning.

The group of four walked together as far as Parade Gardens and Melanie kissed Sebastian goodnight arranging to meet again the following day. Sebastian suggested he get her a cab but it was a warm evening and Melanie was quite happy to walk the rest of the way home. She headed off along Bridge Street and waved off Sebastian as he, Theo and Denis departed along Pultney Bridge.

The streets were quiet and she saw very few people walking along, in fact during the lengthy police investigation that followed the attack, there would be no clear reported sightings of Melanie walking home.

Melanie walked without a care in the world, thinking about going to Greece with Sebastian and enjoying the chilled-out holiday she was going to have, her life was all going so well. She made good time walking up Lansdown Road and when she came to the end, she crossed the road to continue along Camden Row.

It is at this point that I have to give my views on the probable events. Melanie would have had no idea her attacker was lying in wait. I believe the attacker was waiting halfway up Camden Row due to the secluded nature of this location. Melanie hadn't thought about how quiet and dimly lit this short uphill lane was, she had walked this way so often, she gave it no second thought.

It all happened so quickly, he was stood in the shadows in a small area of grass by some garages, possibly reading pages of a soft porn magazine. (Some magazines were recovered at this location). He had noticed Melanie with her shoulder-length blond hair blowing in the wind. She was getting closer, so he slowly reached into his trouser pocket and wrapped his hand around the handle of his knife. Why he was carrying the knife in his pocket is anyone's guess, was this the first time he had a knife and used it? Would it be the last time or might he get the desire to repeat his actions? He had never seen Melanie before but he knew immediately that she was to be his victim. Would it result in her death or would he let her go to re-live the attack, time and time again for the rest of her life? He didn't have to decide now, he would just see what happened.

She was seconds away from being his victim. It all happened so fast, he jumped out as she passed and immediately swung his left arm around her neck and pressed the point of the knife into the small of her back, her immediate reaction was to scream loudly. *"Don't move, I've got a knife"* he said with a low eerie voice. Melanie had not seen him at all, he had grabbed her from behind and she was held so tightly that she could hardly breathe let alone move. *"Please don't hurt me, please"* she said. He was in no mood for chatting and told her to shut up and just do what he said. He made it quite clear that if she made a sound, it would be the last thing she ever did. He now had to take her to the quiet little spot he had earlier identified when he sat in wait. A few jabs in the back with the knife made Melanie comply. (The minor stab wounds found in Melanie's back were consistent with a prodding in the back to make her comply and move). As they got to the top of the road, still holding firmly on to her arm and with the knife pressed into her back, he noticed a camper van driving up the road towards them. *"You just behave normally as if were just chatting"* he said, *"If you arouse any suspicions, your dea*d". The camper van pulled up in the road and the male driver looked across directly towards them.

In fear for her life Melanie did not look across at the van, she stared directly at her attacker and prayed nothing happened to upset him. It seemed like ages before the camper van drove on and Melanie was strangely relieved. The ordeal continued as Melanie was taken to her attacker's prearranged lair, she was soon forced to the floor and made to lie on her back. She had now seen his face and was it at this point that he decided she had to die. He also had to satisfy his sexual needs first but that had been a close shave with the camper van and he could not afford to be caught.

Camden Row, Bath

St Stephens Road where Camper van man saw Melanie and attacker

Rage suddenly came over him, had he already decided she had to be killed? Why wait any longer. The first stab was direct to her chest and almost certainly penetrated the heart. He then lost control and the stabbing blows rained down on Melanie, mainly concentrated around the chest. The pathologist would later count a total of twenty-six separate stab wounds.

Melanie was now bleeding heavily and the blood was soaking into her clothing. The attacker had calmed down and looked at Melanie's lifeless body on the ground. Was she already dead? He had no idea but what he did know was that his sexual urges had not been sated. He undid her blood-stained trousers and pulled them off, knocking her shoes off at the same time, he then removed her blood-stained knickers, he was no doubt aroused on seeing her naked body and wanted to have sex. He forced Melanie's mouth open and inserted his erect penis into her, due to the moist warmth of her mouth he almost immediately ejaculated, he then tried to vaginally penetrate her, but his ejaculate was going on her groin region, clothing and inside her. He fumbled with her bra, his annoyance building again but did not have the patience to unhook it so tugged hard to remove it. The rage subsided as quickly as it had started and he sat back looking at his evil work.

He knew he hadn't got much time because Melanie had screamed when he first approached and he had been seen by the man in the camper van but he could not leave his victim's half naked body at this chosen spot. He quickly re-dressed her by pulling on her trousers and zipping them back up. He put her shoes back on and then realised that he had forgotten the knickers, he didn't have the time to start over again, he needed to tidy things up and move Melanie to another place where she could be found in the morning. He wasn't one of those killers that believed in burying their victims in a hope they would not be found, he felt he was considerate and wanted the girl's family to have closure. He did not want to leave her knickers behind, he grabbed them and then lifted Melanie's body and carried her around the corner where he left her on her back on a tarmac road by a block of garages. He thought it a was an amusing coincidence that he had first approached her by garages in Camden Row and he was now leaving her by garages in a nearby cul-de-sac, St Stephens Court.

Deposition site

He was nearly done now, all he had to do was dispose of her blood-stained knickers or should he keep them as a trophy. He picked the knickers up and took them with him out of St Stephens Court and in his hurry brushed against the wall as he turned left into St Stephens Road. (A blood-stained smear on the wall leaving a tell-tale sign). He planned now to throw the knickers a little way up St Stephens Road rather than keep them, thinking it would make the police believe that he lived in that general direction and send them off on the wrong track. He had never been caught by the police for any crime in the past and believed that he was cleverer than them. He knew though, that the police would not give up easily.

St Stephens Road with knickers on the pavement

He returned to have one last look at Melanie's body before running off right along St

Stephens Road in the opposite direction. He soon realised that he had a cut on his hand which must have been caused during his frantic stabbing. He had dripped a few spots of blood on the pavement during his escape but realised he would have to prevent any more evidence linking him to the area. He found it hard running with one hand in his trouser pocket, stemming the blood drips but felt it more important to stem the drops of blood than running full pelt dripping blood everywhere.

He knew the area quite well having lived in Bath and near to Landsdown for his entire life, he headed straight for a steep flight of steps that led off St Stephens Road down to Camden Crescent as this was a secluded spot where he could avoid any police cars arriving if the screams had been heard.

Steps from St Stephen's Road where attacker ran

As he approached the steps, he saw walking towards him, the driver of the camper van. "*Just had an argument with your girlfriend?*" the man asked. "*Yes*" he replied. He had now been seen twice by this man who had recognised him as being with Melanie earlier, does he stab him as well or just run as fast as he can to escape? He chose the second option and ran full speed down the steep stairs. He needed both hands out of his pockets for this descent even if it meant he was dripping more blood.

He was far enough away from where Melanie's body lay so the police would never link the two together. As he reached the bottom of the stairs, there was a lit streetlight, he had a quick look at his hand and could see he had a small gash on his finger but was happy that he would not need any medical attention and that a plaster when he got home would be enough. (A cluster of blood spots were later found below this streetlamp). He then ran off again along Camden Crescent and all the way home, which only took eight minutes. He was now safe. His pregnant girlfriend was in bed fast asleep so he hunted out a plaster for his finger, had a quick wash down to freshen up and went to bed as if nothing had happened. He lay there a little while not worried about what he had just done or even sorry for his victim, he was thinking whether he had left any clues behind. He changed his thoughts to his girlfriend and wondered whether her being pregnant was the reason for his sexual drive being so high at the moment, he didn't dwell on it for long and fell asleep as if it had been just a normal night.

When he woke up about 9:00am his girlfriend said nothing and didn't even notice his plaster. This was too easy but he would have to follow the police investigation on the news. He was sure that things would go as they usually did with weeks or months of police media reports and the case would then be filed as undetected.

At 5:35am on the Saturday 9th June 1984, Anthony Noonan and his 14-year-old son were delivering milk in the Lansdown area of Bath when they came across the body of Melanie by the garages in St Stephens Court. Mr Noonan, although initially thinking it was a mannequin, realised quickly that it was the body of a young female. He checked for a pulse but he already knew he would not find one, he ran to a neighbouring premise and called the police.

Found besides the body was a keyring with a carved wooden fob attached to it bearing the name Melanie.

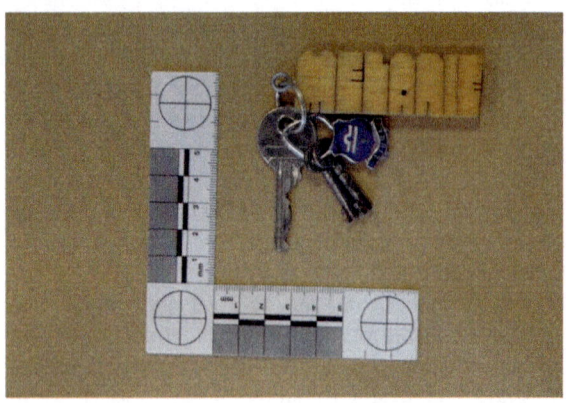

Melanie's keys found on wall at deposition site

The Lansdown area was not a thoroughfare and it was felt by the police that anyone found there must be local. In order to identify the body, the police made the decision to drive around the area with a megaphone and called out the name Melanie, asking anyone who knew a Melanie that was missing from home to come forward. Jean Road heard the announcement and terror immediately took over her body. She ran out into the street and stopped the police vehicle by thumping on the rear wing, she needed to tell them that her daughter Melanie had not returned home the previous night. The reality of the situation sunk in and Jean later stated, *"From that moment, all hell let loose and I knew my daughter was never coming home again."* She went on to identify the body of her loving daughter Melanie and had the images of her dead daughter etched into her mind until the day she died.

It was now 6am and Detective Chief Inspector Malcolm Hughes was sleeping soundly. He had been out until 2:00am celebrating the retirement of one of his sergeants after 30 years service; any excuse for a few drinks with the lads. Malcolm, 'Ginger' to his mates, was a man in his mid 50's, he was stocky build, had a ruddy complexion as well as a full head of bright ginger hair. He was a married man with children of his own, he had been a policeman for 27 years. He was one of Avon and Somerset Constabulary's experienced SIO's and he knew immediately when the phone rang that something serious had happened overnight, most likely a murder. He reached across to pick up the phone and was instantly wide awake as the murder scene was described to him. He realised that he was going to be working long hours for several weeks and would feel the pressures of solving what was apparently a horrendous murder. He gave his wife a kiss on the cheek and said, "*I'll see you when I see you*" and headed off to Bath where he needed an incident room set up. He was going to need his most experienced and trusted staff for this case so as soon as he got in, he started making phone calls. He knew Bath quite well having worked there in the early years of his service but he would need a good mix of officers who knew the area and who were good investigators. Malcolm was going to attend the scene but he wanted the assistance of several experts in their own field. He wanted Dr Kennard who was a Home Office Pathologist who had a mass of experience in murder cases and he would get the most from the post mortem which would take place later that day. His most senior Scene of Crime Officer was John 'Tony' Smith who was a Chief Inspector about the same age as him but who had specialised in assessing and examining scenes of major crimes. Tony would have a team of scenes of crime officers at his disposal to do the work on the ground and Tony could be trusted to organise all that, leaving Malcolm to think about the other aspects of the investigation.

It was 7:30am and Tony had recently woken up and was downstairs making a cup of tea for his wife to drink in bed. It was a beautiful sunny morning and he was looking forward to the family day he had planned with his wife and children. The plan was for a walk around Ashton Park followed by lunch at the Smythe Arms. He should normally have his weekends free but had been called in and worked three of the last five weekends. The phone rang so he casually walked with cup of tea in hand into the hall to answer it. He instantly recognised Malcolm's voice. "*Not again*" he said, Malcolm explained the situation and Tony knew he had no option but to head in to work and he knew at least this weekend and possibly others were going to be cancelled. Tony agreed to contact all the CSI staff he would require and said he would also arrange for the Forensic Scientist; he already had people in mind, his most experienced CSIs Bob and Ray and knew that the best Forensic Biologist for this case would be Mike Rogers, even though he would have to travel from Wales where he lived near to the laboratory in Chepstow, it would be worth the wait to get his expertise. Tony was not at all surprised that all three of them were on days off but they agreed to come in to work because of the murder. They all planned to meet at Bath Police station for a quick briefing and would then visit the crime scene together. There was no immediate rush as the weather was fine and the scene had been secured to preserve any evidence, lots of which may have been invisible to the naked eye.

Malcolm contacted the Coroner's Officer and got the authority to call out Dr Kennard. He was a man in his late 60's who had attended the majority of murder scenes in the Southwest during the past 30+ years. It would be his job to decide on the cause of death.

At about 9:30am, the deposition site was attended by Malcolm Hughes as the Deputy Senior Investigating Officer, Mike Rogers the Forensic Scientist, Dr Kennard the Pathologist, Tony Smith the lead CSI and his Scenes of Crime Officers Bob and Ray. They were faced with a fully clothed body lying on her back with her left leg bent at right angles and left arm outstretched. There were clearly multiple stab wounds to the front and back, which could be seen as cuts in the girl's clothing. There was very little blood at the scene, with only a small pool on the floor. The girl's clothing was however heavily saturated. It was noted that the clasp on her bra was damaged and that her trousers appeared to have been poorly fastened. Blood spots had been found on her shoes as well as on her foot indicating that at some point Melanie's shoes had been off, whilst she was dripping blood. Tony decided, that as the body was not to be removed immediately, it would be necessary to erect a scenes of crime tent around the body. This blue and white striped tent would feature on numerous TV appeals in the weeks to come. Then Ray and Bob videoed the scene and took a series of photographs to preserve the evidence before anything was touched.

The victim's knickers had been found by the first officer who attended the scene where the attacker had left them in St Stephens Road. In order to preserve them, he placed a large black plastic bag over the top of them followed by a cardboard box. The officer had used police tape to cordon off the whole of St Stephens

Court and had taped off a small area around where the knickers were located.

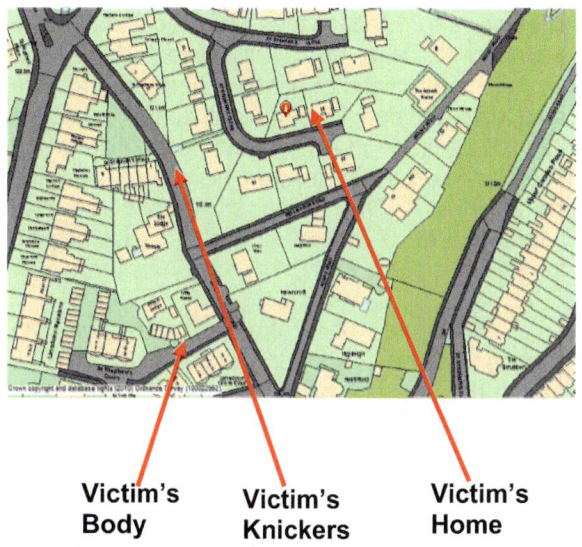

Victim's Body   **Victim's Knickers**   **Victim's Home**

Mike Rogers when assessing the scene, quickly identified what examinations would be necessary before the body was removed. This would involve swabbing some areas of staining as well as taping hands and clothing. He used a strong wide Sellotape to dab on areas being examined which would collect hairs, fibres and any other debris such as skin flakes that would otherwise be lost when the body was moved. Numerous tapings were taken, placed on acetate sheets to trap in the evidence. All tapings and swabs were individually sealed and labelled to preserve the integrity of the evidence. Mike was annoyed when he was shown the knickers and thought that he would need to ensure police training was updated. He was concerned that preserving the knickers under a black plastic bag in the stifling heat might possibly affect the success of blood testing he intended to carry out. Mike directed the CSI team regarding samples he wished them to take and also decided to carry out some swabbing himself in order that he could return to his lab later that same day to start his forensic testing immediately. The police samples could well take a further 24 hours before they arrived at the lab.

Malcolm had already called on the services of the Force Crime Squad officers to attend the Lansdown area to make initial house to house enquiries in the vicinity of the body deposition site and the houses near to where the knickers had been located, in a hope of identifying witnesses who may have heard or seen something during the previous evening.

A Senior Investigating Officer, Detective Superintendent Tim Hurford was allocated to head the enquiry and he remained in charge with Malcolm Hughes as his deputy. It was not until many months into the investigation that Malcolm Hughes was asked to become the SIO due to his knowledge of the case and he continued to do this at the rank of Detective Superintendent until his early retirement due to ill health.

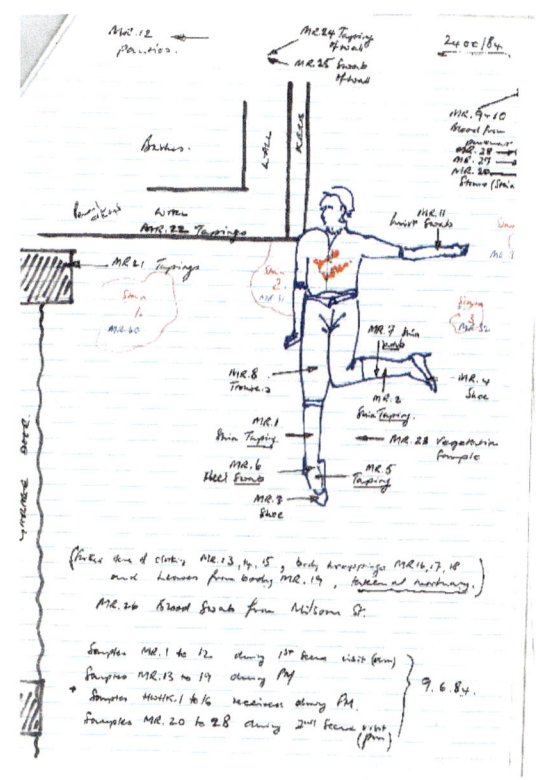

Forensic Scientists scene notes

Blood trail

       A number of blood spots were found on the roadway and pavement in St Stephen's Court, and they appeared to form a trail either into or away from the body. Due to the limited CSI resources available, two of the Crime Squad detectives were diverted from the house-to-house duties and given on the job training on how to carry out presumptive blood tests on spots, this would confirm if any spots located were in fact blood or some other substance. The detectives were then tasked with following the potential blood trail as far as they could. They would be expected to test each spot they found and if it proved positive for blood to circle it in yellow wax crayon, number it for later swabbing by a trained CSI. Little did they know the importance of their job and the fact that they were not only swabbing a trail of the victim's blood spots but also a trail of the offender's blood. They, in fact, identified a total of 85 blood spots as the trail was followed along St Stephens Road, down the steps and along Camden Crescent. Each of the spots was separately swabbed and numbered before being submitted to the Forensic Science Service for analysis in the days to follow. Each of the spots was marked on a street plan so once they were identified, their significance would become apparent.

It was at this point that a smear of blood was also found on the wall where the attacker has brushed against it during his escape. This too was swabbed.

The post-mortem was conducted at Bath hospital by Dr H W H Kennard. He identified a total of 26 stab wounds, several of which could have been fatal. He concluded that the cause of death was haemorrhage due to stab wounds.

The stab wounds were consistent with the cuts in Melanie's clothing suggesting that she was fully clothed at the time she was stabbed. As part of the post-mortem process, each item of the victim's clothing was separately seized and packaged up for forensic testing. Several intimate samples were also taken. These included vaginal, rectal and oral swabs. Dr Kennard was able to indicate that the weapon used appeared to have been a single edged knife with a blade of a minimum length of 4 ½" and a maximum width of 1 ¼". The injuries to Melanie's back were superficial and it was suggested that these injuries may have been as the result of the offender jabbing Melanie in the back to make her comply and move to a different location.

In 1984 the forensic science techniques available to Mike Rogers were much more limited than they currently are. DNA was many years from even being discovered so only blood grouping could be considered. Mike started by screening all the clothing for blood and semen and the intimate swabs were also screened for semen. The technique available for testing bodily fluids such as semen and blood was known as PGM blood grouping (Phosphoglucomutase) and could provide the ABO blood group of any sample as well as an additional PGM figure measuring protein in the sample.

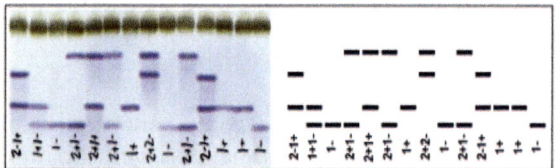

PGM Blood testing

Your blood type is based on whether or not certain proteins are in your red blood cells. These proteins are called antigens. Blood is often grouped according to the ABO blood typing system. The 4 major blood types are: Type A, Type B, Type AB or Type O

The results would hopefully be able to differentiate between the victim's blood and the offender's blood, but Mike knew it would never be able to positively identify an offender. His results would however enable the police to eliminate many suspects but not prove an individual's guilt as it could not discriminate sufficiently.

Mike started his meticulous testing and the results started to come together to form a picture of what had occurred which hopefully would assist in closing in on the offender.

The victim's knickers were tested and there was no trace of any semen found, they were heavily blood stained and numerous areas of blood were tested and found to be blood group A PGM 1+1-. Mike was relieved that he had successfully obtained grouping results from this exhibit bearing in mind the black plastic bag it had been preserved under. This blood result was hardly surprising to Mike as the victim's blood group was also blood group A PGM 1+1-. No other blood group was found on this item and the investigators' view was that the knickers recovered were almost certainly Melanie's and they must have been removed prior to her being sexually assaulted and not worn after the sexual assault, hence no semen. How they came to be up the road in St Stephens Road was causing a lot of questions to be asked.

- Had she been attacked, sexually assaulted and injured, got herself dressed in a panic, hence her clothes being poorly fastened and run off with her knickers possibly stemming blood flow with the knickers in her hands?

- Had the offender taken the knickers?

- It was even considered the possibility of a fox having run off with the discarded knickers after the attack. An expert in fox behaviour would later rule out the idea that a fox had taken the knickers from the scene.

- The knickers were found only 200 yards from Melanie's home so if she had dropped her knickers, why was her body then found 400 yards from her home?

Would the investigators ever find out?

The smear of blood on the wall at the junction of St Stephens Court with St Stephens Road was found to be blood group A PGM 1+1-, again the victim's blood group, so had she put it there when running off or had the offender transferred the victim's blood from blood-soaked clothing on to the wall via his own hand?

The victim's blouse, cardigan and bra were all heavily blood stained and the only blood group found was the victim's blood. Mike also confirmed that the cuts in the material matched the stab wounds to the body proving that Melanie had been clothed at the time of being stabbed. No semen was found on the upper clothing.

Next Mike concentrated on the victim's trousers; these were also heavily blood stained with the victim's blood. They did however reveal semen in the area of the zip. Mike tested this semen and found it to be of blood group A PGM 2-1+. This particular blood group, Mike was able to state was present in only three per cent of the male population so would be very useful to eliminate people. Things were getting more exciting for Mike now as he was starting to get results that may help in proving the offence against a suspect.

It was a well-recognised fact that the majority but not all murders were committed by someone known to the victim, so Malcolm decided that it was going to be necessary to eliminate Melanie's boyfriend Sebastian, her family and friends as well as any other sexual partners she may have had. Malcolm needed to arrange a system of identifying people for elimination and to then get saliva and hair samples in order to forensically eliminate them on blood grouping. Sebastian, his brother Theo, Adrian Road (Melanie's brother) and Anthony Road (Melanie's father) all provided saliva and hair samples and were eliminated.

Mike Rogers then turned to the victim's intimate samples, which also provided extremely strong evidence. Semen was found on Melanie's vaginal swabs and oral swabs; this was of the same blood group as the semen on the trousers namely blood group A PGM 2-1+. He was satisfied that the presence of the semen in the mouth indicated that oral intercourse had taken place shortly before or even after Melanie's death, so this supported the suggestion that it was the offender's semen and not a person Melanie had had consensual intercourse with that evening. Mike reported back to the police that he had identified the offender's blood group.

His attention turned to the 85 blood spots that appeared to form a trail to or from the body. A large number of these blood spots were forensically tested for blood grouping to establish if they were the victim's blood group, the offender's blood group or some other third person. If they were neither, victim nor offender it would be necessary to identify who they belonged to, as the defence would certainly want to use their existence to place doubt in a jury's mind.

Some of the spots tested failed to give any result which was only to be expected but those that did reveal a blood group began to form a pattern that would prove to be very significant.

All the spots giving a result in St Stephens Court and a few leading down St Stephens Road were found to be blood group A PGM 1+1-. These were clearly the victim's blood dripping to the ground as she walked to or was carried into St Stephen's Court. Mike identified a total of 11 spots as being the victim's blood group and spot 45 on the street plan was the one furthest down St Stephens Road that was identified as the victim's.

A total of 14 spots on the blood trail were identified as being from blood group A PGM 2-1+ so were considered likely to be the offender's blood. These spots consisted of 2 in St Stephens Road, numbers 40 and 47, (These were on either side of the victim's blood spot 45), four spots going down the steps and a further 5 along Camden Crescent were also of the offender's blood group. The last offender blood spot being halfway along the crescent. The police were now convinced that they knew the direction that the offender left the scene and they knew the offender's unusual blood group. Mike decided to mark all the blood spots that he had identified with blood grouping and chose to use 'Orange' for the victim's blood group, 'Green' for the offender's group and use other colours for the untested or negative results. Mike had no idea that by doing this the offender's blood would become known as 'Green blood' within the police enquiry. There was one patch of blood that was identified in Landsdown Road that, when grouped, was as a totally different blood group and would need to be eliminated.

Malcolm extended the house-to-house parameters to cover the whole route of the blood trail in order that every house on that route and slightly beyond were visited and the occupants spoken to. Knowing the route also gave Malcolm the opportunity to arrange extensive searches in case the offender had discarded his knife. He knew that if the knife was found this could be another lead to trace the offender, even the possibility of fingerprints that could be searched nationally. Specialist search officers with scythes covered vast overgrown areas of land and 24 knives believe it or not were found. Each knife that fitted the measurements provided by Dr Kennard was examined for blood and every one was eliminated.

There were months and months of police investigation, 94 people were arrested on suspicion of the murder and most were eliminated as their blood group did not match the offender's group. The forensic laboratory was also able to provide 19 names of people known to have blood group A PGM 2-1+ from submissions to the lab in other cases and these were each alibied and eliminated as much as possible.

Months of media appeals failed to identify the offender, posters were put up all around Bath and short video trailers were played in the local cinemas. Malcolm wanted to make sure that every resident in Bath heard about this horrendous attack and pleas for any witness or people who suspected someone of the crime were invited to come forward. All information was followed up and hundreds of people supplied saliva and hair samples and in some cases blood samples.

The attacker I'm sure kept himself up to date with developments in the investigation by watching the news each day. He wanted to keep ahead of the game in case anything led the police to his door. He knew about the house-to-house enquiries and was happy in the knowledge that he lived about half a mile outside the house-to-house area. He also knew that the police would not find his knife because he had washed it and kept it. He had always liked this knife and wasn't going to give it up. Perhaps he was a little disappointed that the media had not given him one of their titles such as 'The Bath Beast' or 'The Slasher.' He was quietly confident and as time went on, with no offender's description being published, he was sure that the mysterious camper van driver had not come forward to explain what he had witnessed. The trail turned cold and with all reasonable lines of the investigation having been exhausted, Malcolm made the difficult decision to submit a closing report and sent the case for filing and classification as a cold case.

When cases were filed like this the Forensic Science Service stored away the evidential swabs, tapings and samples in their archive fridges and freezers. The scientists knew they had done the best possible and could only hope that forensic techniques in the future may help identify this dangerous man. Melanie's clothing was returned to the police in sealed bags and placed into storage where they sat awaiting the day they might prove useful again.

Undetected murder cases are never closed and Malcolm knew that this case would be subject to periodic reviews. What saddened him was that he would soon be retiring and having lived this case every day for over a year,

he had really wanted it detected before his
retirement.

Chapter 2:

Melanie Early Periodic Reviews

Lots would happen over the years when reviews took place and each review would take the case one step closer to being detected.

By 1995 forensic techniques had developed significantly and DNA was a recognised method of identifying offenders from DNA profiles obtained from crime scene stains. All police forces were revisiting 'cold cases' to establish if there was any chance of DNA technology being used to further their investigations. The murder of Melanie Road was no different and it was made subject of a forensic review. The Forensic Science Service were asked to re-test scene stains from the Melanie Road murder investigation using the current SGM (Second Generation Multiplex) DNA technology, looking at DNA alleles to produce a profile. Mike Rogers was still working at the laboratory and he worked with colleagues that had an expertise in DNA. Malcolm Hughes had retired by this stage so a new SIO was asked to oversee the results of any forensic findings.

The victim's oral swab was re-examined and a partial DNA profile was obtained. Partial profiles are where not all the alleles could be identified as opposed to a full profile where all the alleles are established. This would be of limited use because only a near full profile would give the police the ability to identify an offender. Mike and his team re-examined the victim's high vaginal swab which had previously tested positive for semen but no DNA profile at all could be ascertained this time, possibly due to the degrading of the swab over time or due to the limited amount material available. He moved on to the victim's external vaginal swab and a full DNA profile was obtained. This was an exciting development for him, because with a full offender profile, the investigation team could load this onto the National DNA database of offender profiles and await a match. Surely this evil man must be on the database and it would only be a matter of time before his identity was known. A week passed and back came the result that the offender was not on the national DNA database so he had not been arrested and DNA swabbed before. What else could be done with this DNA profile?

The SIO decided he would firstly test the 19 males previously identified with 'Green' blood group type as they had only been eliminated by alibi. It was essential to do this because alibis rely upon the honesty of the alibi witness and they could lie to protect their loved one. With an offender DNA profile, the police could now re-contact and obtain a voluntary DNA swab from the 19 males to eliminate them forensically. It would also be possible for any other person identified as potential suspects to be forensically eliminated on the SGM DNA profile evidence. The full DNA offender profile from the scene could be loaded onto the National DNA database permanently so if the offender were to be swabbed in the future following arrest for another matter, his DNA would flash up as a match and he could then be arrested for Melanie's murder.

Not being satisfied with the full profile from the external vaginal swabs, Mike also re-examined Melanie's trousers in the area of the crotch where the positive semen stain had been found. This resulted in another partial DNA profile.

What was satisfying for Mike was that the partial DNA profiles from the oral swab and the trousers both matched the relevant DNA alleles from the external vaginal full DNA profile. This ruled out any possibility of there having been two unrelated offenders and indicated it was likely to have been only one offender. There were no loose ends for the defence to use in any future trial.

The SIO decided to have a renewed press appeal as it was 11 years since the offence and he hoped he could encourage people to come forward with suggestions of offenders knowing the forensic evidence could prove or disprove that person's guilt.

It was following a press appeal that there was a call received in the incident room suggesting Gordon Charles should be considered as a suspect for the murder of Melanie Road. He was a local man who had previously been convicted of the murder of an elderly woman. He was known to have blood group A PGM 2-1+. Charles had supplied DNA when he was arrested for the murder of the elderly woman and the results had indicated that he could not be excluded as the murderer of Melanie Road even on DNA evidence. He was arrested and denied the offence and had given an alibi which had been confirmed by a family member.

There was something concerning the SIO which made him cautious about the forensic evidence. The DNA taken from Charles had been taken using an old DNA technique, so it now had to be upgraded to the SGM DNA currently being used. All that was needed was a new swab from Charles to prove his guilt and end the uncertainty about who killed Melanie. Surprisingly, Charles was quite happy to provide his DNA and was told that he would be further interviewed once the results were known. There was several days delay in waiting for the anticipated positive result but at 9:00am, one week after the swab had been taken, a call from the forensic lab was made to the incident room. *'Gordon Charles can be eliminated; he is not your murderer'*. That was not the result that was wanted or expected, everything seemed to point to Charles being the offender up until that point and now the investigation was back to square one.

More media publicity and appeals for witnesses followed and with the mention of offender DNA being released the attacker was getting a little worried. He knew he had never given his DNA before so as long as he kept out of trouble and didn't give his DNA in the future, he should be ok. What he couldn't afford to happen was someone putting his name forward as a suspect as he had learnt about the police doing mass swabbing of suspects. He also thought about 'Camper van man'. Why had he not come forward and given the description? Had he come forward but the police were keeping it quiet? He knew that any names put forward to the public would be followed up and the suspects were being eliminated forensically. The attacker became so concerned he decided that it would be a good idea to move away from the Bath area and chose to move to the adjoining city of Bristol. He was married by this time and had a wife and two children, he could easily explain to them that work as a painter and decorator would be easier to find in the larger city so the family moved, not knowing the real reason.

By 1996 the case was again filed and returned to 'Cold Case' status as every potential lead came to nothing.

In 2000 the SGM DNA processes that had looked at 7 sites (14 alleles) of the DNA profile had been further developed and was now a technique known as SGM+. This looked at 10 sites and a full profile was 20 alleles. This was a much more complete profile and meant that results were even more accurate. The national DNA database had also been updated and arrested people having their DNA taken would produce a 20-allele profile for loading onto the database for comparison against crime scene stains. It was possible to compare SGM profiles against SGM+ but it would be better if the Melanie Road DNA scene profiles could be upgraded to SGM+. A small review team was put together made up of detectives from various departments within the force led by the SIO Rod Hansen. The forensic science service was asked to review all the forensic evidence gathered to date, to decide what further work using SGM+ technology might assist. Mike Rogers had retired so a new forensic advisor Colin Dark had to learn the case intimately.

As the external vaginal swabs had provided the best result, namely a full SGM profile in 1995, Colin decided that they stood the best chance of these swabs being upgraded to SGM+. The remains of the vaginal swabs were brought out of forensic storage and examined again. Only a partial profile (12 alleles) was obtained, this had hardly improved on the 1995 evidence so was disappointing and not a good omen for the further work planned. The high vaginal swabs again gave no DNA profile so this also took the case no further.

The oral swab was the next to be put through the new process and a reasonable partial profile was obtained (14 alleles). It was really a full or almost full profile that would be needed to be loaded onto the national DNA database and in fact only a full profile (20 alleles) would be good enough to use for familial DNA searching that the team hoped to try out. Colin examined the semen stains from Melanie's trousers, these had previously only produced a partial profile but he knew that without trying he had no hope of getting the required full profile.

The semen stains produced a profile (19 alleles), which fell just one short of the target.

In the following years the stains were tested and retested several times and eventually a full profile (20 alleles) was obtained. The team knew that loading this onto the national database would not result in a DNA hit as the previous SGM profile would already have done this but there were advantages on having the full SGM+ profile on the database, least of all the familial searching they so eagerly wanted to try. It was when contacting the database that the team found out, that due to an administrative error, the SGM profile from the murder scene had inadvertently been removed from the database 1 ½ years previously so there were thousands of new profiles on the database that had never been checked against the Melanie Road murder profile. It therefore could be, by simply loading the new SGM+ profile now obtained, that a match would be made straight away, and the offender identified. There was an anxious one-week wait but once again there was great disappointment that no DNA hit was found.

It was also recognised that there was no record of Melanie's DNA profile at the forensic science lab. This would be essential to prove any future case as eliminating her profile from any mixed profiles would clarify results. The forensic archives were contacted and stated that none of the blood samples taken from Melanie during the post-mortem had been retained. A surrogate profile would have to be established by taking profiles from the blood on Melanie's bra and knickers and also taking samples from

Melanie's parents and siblings. It was by going through this process that a full SGM+ surrogate profile was ascertained for Melanie.

Familial DNA searching was a method by which the DNA database would identify people on the national DNA database that could be related to the murderer due to the similarity of their DNA. (Bearing in mind everyone's DNA is made up of 50 per cent their mother's DNA and 50 per cent their father's DNA). Familial searches would identify possible parents or children of the murderer or possible siblings whose DNA was on the database. Familial searching would result in long lists of names being produced showing the most likely at the top of the list. These lists had to be researched by the team. It was necessary to identify any family relative that could be the murderer, trace them, swab them and eliminate them. A few years of voluntary DNA swabbing commenced, but each voluntary swab tested by the forensic scientist proved negative meaning the attacker's identity remained unknown.

Time had now moved on to 2009 and as previously mentioned it was then that Detective Sergeant Julie Mackay had decided that it was time for the review team to take a new look at all the undetected murders again. This included the Melanie Road case. I was not at that time allocated the case to review but I could remember the case when it happened as I had been a young detective at Bishopsworth Police Station in Bristol. I had been dealing with a missing woman Shelly Morgan who had left her home in Bedminster, Bristol on 11th June 1984 to find somewhere to set up and paint the scenery. She never returned home and had not been seen again.

Although I was not involved in Melanie's murder investigation, it had been all over the news and I was quite familiar with it.

Photograph of Shelly Morgan

The body of Shelly Morgan by the way was found partially buried three months later in woodland in Backwell near Bristol. The police in Weston-Super-Mare investigated the murder. She had been stabbed to death multiple times. Due to the fact that this was the murder of a lone female walking outdoors, who was attacked and stabbed to death, and the fact that the murders of Melanie Road and Shelly Morgan were only two days apart and 12 miles apart, it was considered that the murders could have been committed by the same offender.

The Melanie Road murder was the number one priority for the Review Team and as the 25th anniversary of the murder was quickly approaching, it was decided to pursue the investigation in two ways. A Crimewatch reconstruction would give renewed media publicity and generate new lines of investigation. Whilst this was going on, it was also time for a new familial search exercise.

New profiles are added to the National database at a frightening rate and the accuracy of familial results was becoming more reliable. Each name on the familial lists would have a likelihood ratio indicating how similar the profile was to the crime scene profile, taking into account factors like rare alleles.

The Crimewatch programme went out and calls came into the staff monitoring the phones almost immediately. 69 calls were received about the case and these would each need to be followed up. Most of the team went to the Crimewatch studio to take phone calls but I remained in the office to start researching any information. Any person whose name was put forward would have to be eliminated. This could be as simple as confirming that they were already on the national DNA database because if they were, an offender DNA match would already have been reported. Other people would have to be researched and located for a voluntary sample to be taken from them for elimination purposes and if they were already deceased, a relative would have to be identified to assist in elimination.

There were two phone calls received in to the Crimewatch team which are worthy of specific note.

The first call was anonymous, the caller stated that she was a nurse employed at a nursing home in the Surrey area. Some twelve months previous she had been providing palliative care for a patient called Donald Gallagher. He had only weeks to live and he had confided in her that he had killed a girl back in the 1980s in the Southwest area, he had mentioned stabbing and the fact that he had never been caught. The nurse had not taken the confession seriously until she had seen the Crimewatch programme and believed the facts could fit the murder of Melanie Road. A renewed request was put out on the Crimewatch update programme for the nurse to phone back but she never did. I now had to start research to identify Donald Gallagher. Fortunately, the name was not too common but checking deaths in the Surrey area over the previous 2 years did not identify anyone by that name having died, in fact no Donald Gallagher was identified to have died nationally. What I did find was a man called Robert Donald Gallagher aged 58 who had been in a nursing home in Surrey and died 14 months ago. No-one else seemed to fit the information supplied by the anonymous caller, so a team was sent up to the nursing home to make enquiries. This was a fantastic lead and if the nurse could be found and make a statement about the confession, it could be the start of building a case. Despite extensive enquiries, no-one admitted being the caller or having received any confession from Robert Donald

Gallagher. He was described as a quietly spoken man, who was very polite and no problem to the staff. The only way to progress this would be to locate Robert's family and it wasn't long before I had tracked down his wife and daughter. Officers had the unenviable task of approaching Robert's wife to explain the situation and the need to establish his DNA profile to eliminate him or of course prove him to be the murderer. The family were very helpful as they wanted to clear Robert's name. They provided the police with an old pair of his spectacles and the cuff from his blood pressure machine. Both items were submitted for forensic analysis and both revealed the same full SGM+ DNA profiles. The only problem was that the profiles did not match the Melanie Road murder profiles so he was eliminated. At least his family was happy but there were a few sad faces in the review team.

The second interesting call that came into the Crimewatch team was from someone called Ben Schwarzkopf. As the result of the information given, my colleague Alan Andrews and I were dispatched to take a statement from him. Rather than summarising his information below is an extract from his statement:

"*At the end of 1981, I moved from Bournemouth to the City of Bath to live. My parents at that time owned a Coffee and Tea shop in the centre of Bath. I lived at that time in Camden Road, Lansdown, Bath. In 1984, I was the proud owner of a VW Camper van which was light blue in colour with the spare wheel on the front. The VW was a left-hand drive vehicle* which made it difficult for me to park. Parking in the Lansdown area of Bath in 1984 was very difficult at the best of times."

"On Wednesday 10th November 2010, I telephoned the Avon and Somerset Constabulary in relation to events that occurred in the early hours of Saturday morning on the 9thJune 1984. This was due to the fact that I had been suffering with a very disrupted sleep pattern, dreaming about the events that I had witnessed on that morning. My partner persuaded me that I should phone the Police. My call was in relation to the murder of a girl on the 9thJune 1984 which I had always thought was solved."

"On the day I phoned the Police, I went home and looked on the internet for 'Bath Murder.' Initially a murder from 1996 Melanie Hall came up so I put into the search field '9th June 1984' and a murder Crimewatch programme came up with a short video reconstruction of a small group of people leaving a club in Bath. The group split up and a girl went on her own to the Lansdown Road area. I felt that what I had witnessed would be important to the Police."

"I am very certain that the events that I will relate to the Police are the correct date as my 20th birthday was on Monday 11th June 1984. I went out on the Friday night in Bath Centre. This was not much of a celebration as I had to get up very early on the Saturday morning the 9thJune 1984 to work. I met a small group of friends and we went to Moles night club. I did not consume any alcohol that night for two reasons, I was working early the next morning and I was driving my camper van."

"At the end of the evening in the early hours of the morning after 1am, I drove along Upper Bristol Road into Queens Square into George Street, past Broad St and turned left into Lansdown Road driving towards Camden Crescent. As I approached the junction of Camden Crescent, I saw a young woman on her own on the right-hand side of the road walking up the hill almost at the junction. I drove into Camden Crescent looking for somewhere to park my camper van. I was driving slowly and at one point tried to park and even got out of the van to see if I could park. I couldn't get into the space so drove up towards St Stephens Road. I tried again to park in St Stephens Road at a 'kink' in the road, again I failed to park. I manoeuvred around the hairpin bend which I could never do in one turn and drove up the hill in St Stephens Road. I saw a possible space around halfway along this part of St Stephens Road and thought that I would turn around and go back and park. I realised that I would have to drive around the block, into Lansdown Grove, into Lansdown Road, up the hill, back into St Stephens Road and return to the parking space. As I drove up onto the flatter section of the road to my left was a grassed or green area piece of land with a bench. I saw a couple who appeared to be having an argument near the bench where they were standing. Both were standing very close together. I was driving slowly; the area was lit by street lighting. My eyesight then was very good as it still is. As my *vehicle was left-hand drive, I was only 20 to 25 feet from the two people."*

"I believe that the girl I saw at Camden Crescent was the same girl I later saw arguing on the grass area."

"I drove around the block as described above and, on the way back down St Stephens Road, I again saw the same couple in my headlights. They were a few yards up St Stephens Road from the grassed area. The female was in front with the man very close behind. I stopped or nearly stopped beside them, she would have been about a metre from the front offside wing of the camper van facing the man with her back towards the hill. She turned and looked at me. Her face was pasty white. I thought it was just an argument so I drove on and found the parking place and could still hear the couple arguing. I parked my van and got out. This was just before the hairpin bend in St Stephen's Road. As I got out of my vehicle, I heard a woman screaming. I had already walked away from my vehicle around the hairpin bend and into the lower part of St Stephens Road. As the screaming continued, I decided to retrace my steps back towards where I had parked."

"Throughout the minutes I was retracing my steps, I continued to hear the extremely loud screaming. It took me some minutes to get back to my van. I would say that from the very first time that I saw the couple arguing until I parked my van, walked towards my house and returned to the van when the screaming stopped, to be

*between at least 10 and up to 15 minutes in
length."*

*"I waited beside my van for a short
period. I then walked up St Stephens Road
back towards the grass area. There are a
number of steps which join the upper and lower
parts of St Stephens Road. As I got to the top of
these steps, I was confronted by the man who I
had seen arguing with the woman. I said, "Have
you been arguing with your girlfriend?", he
replied "yes". The man appeared agitated and
moving quite quickly. I didn't see anything in his
hands but I had a feeling he had something on
him. This was an impression as I think that only
one of his arms were swinging when he walked.
I got the distinct feeling that I recognised the
man. I cannot remember more than that feeling
I had seen him before this night perhaps in a bar
or club."*

*"The man went down the steps two at a
time. The steps are quite steep and are uneven.
I followed some yards behind as I was interested
in trying to see where he lived. At the bottom of
the steps, he paused briefly then ran into
Camden Crescent, about halfway along the
crescent he began to run even faster. He was
maybe 25 yards in front of me, he went out into
Lansdown Road and went down the hill towards
Bath centre and he then disappeared. I returned
home and went to bed."*

*"I would describe the girl as someone
not older than me. I would say around 18 or 19
years of age. I think she was of slim build and
about 5'3" to 5'5" tall. She had mousey brown*

shoulder length hair and had a pale complexion."

"I would describe the man as around 5'11" tall of slim athletic build. He was older than the girl and me, I think between 20 and 30 years old. He had dark hair quite long over his collar. He was a white male. He wore dark clothing and his arms were covered. I would say casually dressed. He wasn't pale skinned and was not foreign and when he replied to me "Yes" he sounded English."

"On Saturday morning, I got up around 8am to go to work. I walked to my vehicle as I did so, I saw four or five police, white Transit type vans parked in Camden Crescent. I collected my vehicle and drove down St Stephens Road into Camden Crescent. I saw a Police Officer by one of the vans. I stopped and spoke to him. I told him I had seen something earlier that morning. I was not aware there had been a murder. The Police Officer asked where I lived and when I told him, he said that I would be spoken to when Officers called on house-to-house later. The Police never got back to me after that. I cannot remember when I heard that a girl had been murdered but it was perhaps later on that Saturday."

Ben Schwarzkopf described himself as being on the autism scale who, as a young adult, found it difficult to form relationships and would spend lots of time alone, he was not interested in the local news and did not follow it on the radio or television. He displayed some unusual memory traits. He explained that this manifested itself in him by his memory being 'very visual and compartmentalised.' He appeared to still recall some detail of the events of 1984 by creating images like videos playing in his head and appeared to be cognitively interviewing himself, putting himself back in 1984 as he remembered details. Ben stated that he had researched on the internet and knew he was phoning about the Melanie Road murder that occurred in Lansdown in 1984. He had not found out any of the details of the crime reported over the years whilst researching, so his statement was not contaminated by media reports he had seen. It was due to his medical condition that he had not become aware over the years that the murder remained undetected and he had assumed that it had been cleared up because the police never attended at his home during house-to-house enquiries.

I set about researching the original investigation file which had been stored over the years in various locations throughout the force area but was now sat in a warehouse in the Bourneville area of Weston-Super-Mare.

*Police archive storage facility at
Bourneville*

I was able to confirm that Ben's name
was within the system because, in July 1984, he
had phoned the police because he had a
customer in the coffee shop with cuts and
scratches to his face. The police had appealed
to the public for anyone seen with scratches as
they believed it was possible that Melanie had
fought back. The man with scratches was
questioned by the police and eliminated. This
was the only record of Ben Schwarzkopf in the
system. I also checked the house-to-house
records and it became apparent that the
parameters set by Malcolm Hughes once the
green blood trail had been discovered did
include Camden Road but stopped at number 7,
only a few doors short of Schwarzkopf's
address.

If Ben had been fully interviewed in 1984, it is quite likely that he could have produced a photofit of the offender that would have been circulated via the media and possibly someone would have put forward the attacker as a likeness and suspect. That opportunity was missed but bearing in mind Ben's unusual medical condition, Julie Mackay, Alan Andrews and I discussed the possibility of trying to get a photofit now, even after 25 years. The experts at Police HQ would not entertain the idea. Ben was quite a proficient artist and had showed off a number of his artworks to Alan and I when we took his statement. As a last resort, Ben agreed to draw a sketch of the attacker. I was a little disappointed when the sketch arrived as it did not come up to the standard of Ben's other artwork. It was never used by the media, you decide for yourself if it could have assisted.

Camper van man had at last been identified and helped confirm some of the details of the attack on Melanie in 1984. Ben was not able to lead the team to the identity of the offender, so the investigation continued.

Ben Schwarzkopf's sketch of the attacker

Familial searching had been tried on a couple of occasions but in 2011 a new search was commissioned. I was supplied with 4 lists of names from the familial search results, each contained 100 names. The lists were marked up Parent/Child unfiltered, Parent/Child filtered, Sibling unfiltered and Sibling filtered. The filtering referred to geographical filters and age that had been used to limit the results to people that had been swabbed in the Southwest region and whose relative could be of the right age group. The Avon and Somerset constabulary had only once previously had success with familial searching, so I made enquiries with other forces and was told that the majority of the successes had come from the relative in the top ten on the familial list and they recommended not attempting to eliminate relatives from all 100 people on each of the 4 lists. Julie decided that the team should concentrate on the top 30 of each list so this gave 120 new people from the familial lists that had to be researched.

I personally researched all 120 people, to identify any father, son or brother that could be the attacker, the men identified then needed to be forensically eliminated. Some were eliminated as they were already on the national DNA database, but the majority had to be traced, voluntarily swabbed and then eliminated. The Forensic Science Service had gone out of business so a new forensic provider, Cellmark was to be used for all the eliminations. Scientist Mike Wheelhouse had been a forensic biologist for many years and agreed to take the lead.

It did not take too much skill for me to recognise that the top name of the Parent/Child unfiltered list was of significant interest. Trish Blackmore was born in 1976 and her DNA had been taken two years previously when she was arrested for a minor theft offence. The familial list showed the likelihood ratio figure as 44,505.6. The person in position two on this same list had a likelihood ratio of only 17,111.8 in comparison. The ratios alone made Trish Blackmore a 'Screamer'. This was a term used in the familial world where the likelihood ratio figure was so high that it should scream out to investigators that their relative should be considered as a strong suspect. Some of the experts in the forensic world were so convinced with the results, they suggested they would bet their mortgage that Trish's father was the attacker.

I identified Trish's father as Mark Blackmore born in 1958, he had no previous convictions recorded against him. Research identified that he was a painter decorator by trade and currently lived in Colchester but had conducted contract work throughout the country, often staying away from home to complete the contracted job. The only way he could be eliminated was by being approached for a voluntary swab. Officers travelled up to Colchester and were knocking on Mark's door at 6am. Mark was told the reasons for the officers' attendance and that they were investigating a murder in Bath, dating back to 1984. Mark claimed only to have visited Bath once or twice as a tourist but had no knowledge of any murder. He was very reluctant to give a DNA swab because he was concerned that if the familial results were pointing to him as the offender due to his daughter's similar DNA, then could they by, some fluke, indicate him as the attacker. Following an hour of discussions, Mark gave a voluntary DNA swab, and the officers left the address with a smile on their faces and a skip in their step. It was now only a matter of time and the attacker would be in custody and charged with murder.

Cellmark, the forensic provider, agreed at a premium rate to rush through the DNA testing and comparison so within 24 hours they were phoning up Julie with the result. *"I don't believe it, but we have checked it three times and Mark Blackmore can be eliminated"*. Julie was shocked and suggested for completion a sample be taken from Trish's mother just to confirm that Mark was the father and to explain the results. It was right, Mark was Trish's father and was eliminated, another good lead had come to a dead end. Using the DNA taken from Mark Blackmore, we also eliminated his brother Dave as his offending history gave us reasons to want to eliminate him.

The review team attended a regional review officers conference and the subject under discussion was the 'The offender is in the system'. It had been proven statistically that in cold case investigations that had gone on to be detected, the offender's name had been in the investigation for some reason, not necessarily as a suspect. This was in 70 per cent of the cases. When we came back, we had lengthy discussions and we decided that if the offender was amongst the names in the Melanie Road murder investigation, it was only a matter of working meticulously through the names, swabbing people until we had a hit. There was obviously going to be thousands of names in the original investigation, and it was going to be necessary to somehow prioritise who should be swabbed first, this would mean that if the offender was in our system, we would swab him earlier rather than later and save a lot of money. The College of Policing had experience in creating scoring matrixes bespoke to investigations that could help in the prioritisation process.

I attended a meeting with Julie and various experts connected with the College of Policing. These included an analyst, geographical profiler and offender profiler. We had sent them copies of relevant documentation to assist them in coming up with a prioritisation matrix form. What we would have to do was to look at each male person featuring in the investigation and to give them a score based on certain criteria. We had a description of the offender from Ben Schwarzkopf, we had the forensic scientists telling us that the blood grouping and DNA tests had indicated that the offender's ethnicity was most likely to be white, North European and the offender profiler also gave an input about the types of offenders committing this type of offence. This resulted in the highest scores being given to white males aged 18 to 35 years 6' tall or over.

Name:		Nom No:	
1. Criminality		Score	Total
Use only the highest scoring out of a-e			
a) Conviction and/or intelligence information re all theft and kindred offences	8		
OR b) Conviction and/or intelligence information re sexual offending	7		
OR c) Conviction and/or intelligence information re serious assault, common assault, or possession of an offensive weapon	6		
OR d) Conviction and/or intelligence information re offences relating to the police/prison/court, fraud, arson, criminal damage, public disorder or minor traffic	5		
OR e) Conviction of any other kind	2		
	Total (max score 8)		
b or c of above involved a female victim	Add 3		
Any of above involved theft of underwear	Add 3		
Any of above involved use of a knife	Add 3		
	Total (max score 9)		
		Total section 1 – (max score 17)	
2. Age At the time of the offence		Score	Total
18-35 years		14	
36-40 years		10	
	Total (max score 14)		
3. Ethnicity			
EA1 or EA045		16	
EA2 8		8	
	Total (max score 16)		
4. Height			
6' tall or over		5	
	Total (max score 5)		
5. Geography At the time of the offence			
Resident within 5 miles of where body was found		20	
Resident within 5-10 miles of where body was found		10	
OR Had some form of geographic connection or association within 5 miles of where body was found		7	
	Total (max score 20)		
		Total sections 2-5	
OVERALL TOTAL SECTIONS 1-5 (max score 72)			

Prioritisation Scoring Matrix

The offender profiler also suggested that the highest score should be given to people with previous convictions or intelligence for theft and similar offences rather than previous sexual offending. This was quite a surprise to me, but this was based on statistics. Additional scoring was given for offences against women and offences using knives.

The geographical profiler believed that the offender was likely to live, work or have strong links to the area of the crime. People who were resident within 5 miles of where the body had been recovered would score greatest in that section of the form.

The maximum a person could score was 72 points.

The 1984 investigation had been run on a paper system supported by index cards. I understood this system as I had used it several times myself before the introduction of HOLMES (Home Office Large Major Enquiry System). HOLMES was a computerised method of storing all the information gathered during an investigation. We had to do something to make it easier to research the vast amount of information gathered during the initial investigation. Was it now time to transfer the Melanie Road investigation from the paper system onto the computer. It was a massive time-consuming task for a case that had remained undetected for 25 years but if the offender was in the system, it could be managed much better within HOLMES. All the old index cards were with the papers in the Bourneville storage warehouse.

Major incident room

Investigation card index system

As a compromise, Julie agreed that all the 8,267 males (referred to as nominals in the policing world) from the card index would be created within HOLMES. This task would have to go to the Indexers based at the Major Crime Unit and would take well over a year to complete. All the males would then have to be given their matrix score and mass voluntary swabbing would then be carried out.

The review team consisted of only a sergeant and six members of staff which was clearly too small to carry out a mass swabbing exercise. The Major Crime Unit was the obvious team to deal with this and I volunteered to be seconded to the Major Crime Investigation Unit (MCIU) to continue working on the case.

It was an unfortunate time within the MCIU as there was a high volume of complex live murders under investigation within the office. The Melanie Road investigation suffered as a result. Although Sergeants and staff member were identified to work on the case, they were soon deployed on other current murder cases, and I was left alone to keep the case progressing.

Indexers were creating the nominals, one particular indexer Lesley and I almost single-handedly scoring every male nominal. I would then research those scoring more than 50 points to trace and swab them. Those scoring more than 50 were put in the phase one swabbing. No-one was to be eliminated on the scoring system alone. The forensic results continued coming back at a rate of 30 every 2 months and each time the results were negative. Fifty per cent of all the swabbing was carried out by me but others helped if and when the MCIU had any downtime. There was never any

Sergeant to report to but things started to look up because Julie Mackay was promoted to the rank of Detective Inspector and transferred to the MCIU.

Julie and I were teamed up again and she was able to generate more interest from the management team. In order to keep others interested, Julie asked me to identify a monthly target person for elimination. This was not difficult because amongst all the names within the investigation papers were quite reasonable suspects.

I'll give you two examples of the types of person of interest that featured.

Target of the month, Kenneth Brooks was born in 1943, he had been living in Bath at the time of the murder and had links to Lansdown. He left Bath two days after the murder without telling anyone why. One week after the murder, he attacked a 23-year-old woman in the street in London and strangled her until she became unconscious. He told her that she was the second person he had attacked in the past two weeks. Brooks was disturbed during his London attack and ran off but was caught and arrested. The woman survived.

When interviewed, Brooks denied the murder of Melanie Road but claimed that he knew her. It was reported in the paperwork that he was eliminated in 1984 on blood grouping but the results could not be verified. My research showed that Brooks had died in 1998 and in order to forensically eliminate him, it would be necessary to get a voluntary DNA swab from his younger brother Ben. I traced Ben to an address in London, but he refused to give a voluntary swab and continued to refuse for six months until he eventually changed his mind. Y-STR DNA technology looks specifically at an area of the DNA chain that relates to alleles passed down by male to male. Mike Wheelhouse used this to establish that Ben's Y-STR did not match the Y-STR profile from the Melanie Road crime scene stain. Ben's Y-STR would however be identical to his brother Kenneth's Y-STR. Mike could therefore eliminate Kenneth Brooks for the murder of Melanie.

Target of the month, Daniel Baker was born in 1959 and lived in Bath. Rumours from several sources were circulating that he was responsible for the murder of Melanie Road who he knew. Daniel took his own life on 7th July 1984 by hanging himself. The only method of forensically eliminating Daniel now, was to obtain a voluntary DNA swab from Daniel's brother Noel who I found was still living in Bath. Noel had never been able to understand why his brother had taken his own life and was not sure what to do. He wanted to help in proving his brother's innocence but was also concerned that by giving his DNA, it could prove his brother's guilt. He was given time to think it over and discuss with other family members and between them they agreed to help. Julie and I had learnt that there was no point in getting our hopes up and as expected, Mike Wheelhouse yet again eliminated one further person.

There were very few occasions when men refused to give their DNA sample for elimination and some that initially did were persuaded to reconsider their decision by reading a letter written by Jean explaining why they should help the police. I will quote a passage from her letter. *' People have said to our family, let it rest and move on with your lives. We can't, I'm not sure if we will ever heal whilst the perpetrator still walks the street, getting on with his life, leaving the Road family's life in limbo. We mourn for Melanie every day and night.'*

Time was passing, people were being eliminated and Julie was being put under pressure to file the case once more. Could Julie convince the management team to pay for one more familial run? It was now 2015 and thousands more names had been added to the database. She put forward a strong case but monies were tight. The offender would now be in his 60's or 70's and may even be dead. The senior management team were making comments such as:

'If we haven't got a DNA match or familial match by now, we are not going to get one.'

'You are just flogging a dead horse.'

Julie and I were convinced that we could succeed if we were given the chance. The offender had to be brought to justice for Melanie's sake and her family.

Chapter 3:

New attempt at Familial DNA
May 2015

I was quite happy when Julie told me that she had obtained agreement for one further familial run. I knew how much they cost, taking into account the number of voluntary swabs that the new work would generate. Headquarters were being difficult about the amount of money being spent on operation Rhodium. She had no doubt needed to use all her powers of persuasion to get it authorised. I also knew that I would get four more lists of 100 names and introduce many more people for swabbing, but I was used to that by now. There was still little help from the MCIU due to their other commitments and nearly all the swabbing was now being done by myself with the occasional one or two being done by others.

It has been said by some that we were lucky with this familial run but I am a strong believer that luck comes to those people that deserve it. The luck surrounded the fact that there was an administrative error which resulted in the familial run being delayed by six months so, when it was chased up and carried out, thousands of additional names were now on the database and included in the search process.

The time arrived on the evening of 27th May 2015 when I received my 4 new lists via an email. The lists did not contain any likelihood ratios possibly because they wished to get the information to us quicker, having already delayed by six months. The names were however in order of the most likely on top.

As soon as I viewed the Parent /Child unfiltered list, I recognised the name Trish Blackmore but what was a surprise to me was that it was in position 2. That meant that the name at the top of the list was an even better match and would have a greater likelihood ratio than 44,505.6. I immediately started my research on the name Clare Hampton. She was born in Bath in 1972 and on 10th of September 2014 she had an argument with her boyfriend and hit out at him breaking his neck chain. Clare had been arrested and cautioned for criminal damage, but the important thing was that the officer dealing with her took her fingerprints and DNA sample. It was that DNA sample that resulted in Clare being in position 1 on my familial list. This is where our luck came in, because it was apparent that had we not had the six months delay due to the administrative error, the familial run would have been carried out before Clare Hampton had even given her DNA sample so she would not have been number one on our list.

Due to Clare's age, it was her father that I was interested in and within half an hour I had identified Clare's father as Christopher John Hampton born in Bath in 1952. I now set about trying to locate him and established that he had no previous convictions. There were no Christopher John Hamptons living in Bath, so I opened my research to further afield. I identified two who lived in Bristol but neither lived with the woman I had identified as Clare's mother. I had already located Clare Hampton and obtained her mobile phone number. As was normal, there was no-one to ask and Julie was heavily involved in another case so I made the decision to phone up Clare and ask about her father. I knew Julie well enough to know that she would be happy with that course of action.

I spoke with Clare Hampton and explained that I was investigating the murder of Melanie Road in 1984. She had only been 12 years old at the time so had no idea how she could be of any assistance. I went on to explain that her DNA had some similarities to the offender's DNA, so I was wishing to get in contact with her father to eliminate him. To reassure her, I explained that I had lists containing 400 names of people with similar DNA and hers was only one. Clare was a little embarrassed because her stupid argument with her boyfriend was now going to cause her father inconvenience. Clare supplied her father's address and phone numbers explaining that he was re-married and had a new family. She had little contact with him, but he knew all about her being arrested and she was quite happy with me talking to her dad about it. I even gave Clare the option of contacting her father first to let him know that the police wanted to speak to him.

Clare declined the offer saying that she was too embarrassed. Ten minutes after finishing the call to Clare, I was on the phone to Christopher Hampton.

I introduced himself to Christopher stating that I was a Crime Investigator engaged in a cold case investigation into the murder of Melanie Road in Bath in 1984. I explained that the reason I had phoned him was because his daughter Clare's DNA, that was taken following her argument with her boyfriend, had been loaded onto the national DNA database and it was found to be similar to the DNA of the person who murdered Melanie Road. I again explained that I had lists containing 400 names of people with similar DNA and Clare's was only one amongst many. I then asked if I could possibly take a voluntary DNA swab from him in order to eliminate him from my enquiries. As was my normal practice, I explained that the taking of a DNA swab was voluntary, it would only take up to 15 minutes of his time and could be done at home, at work, at a police station or even sat in a car in a carpark. Christopher agreed and stated that there was a carpark outside where he was working as a painter decorator in Ashton, Bristol. Since my retirement as a police officer and having taken up a position as a crime investigator I had chosen to reduce my working hours and was working only Monday to Thursday each week. As it was Thursday 28th May, I made an appointment to see Christopher at 10:00am on the Monday, when I was next on duty.

At 7:00am on Monday 1st June, I arrived at work and signed out a plain car to use for the three people I was planning to swab that day. I was due to start with Christopher Hampton and then travel to Wales and swab Gerry Jones to assist in eliminating all his brothers. Gerry had been in position three on the Parent/Child and Sibling list and the research into him discovered that he had three brothers and a father that needed eliminating. His father was deceased and, more interestingly, his eldest brother had at some time in the mid 1980's, left Wales to go to Scotland following rumours he had killed someone. Gerry's brother could not be located but Gerry was happy to provide a DNA sample which could be used to eliminate all his brothers and father in one go. I got together 5 sealed swab kits.

At 9.50 am, I arrived in the carpark at Liberty House, South Liberty Lane, Ashton. I telephoned Christopher Hampton on his mobile and two minutes later saw him approach the police car. Christopher was a 63-year-old male of stocky build, ruddy complexion and about 5'8" tall. He had short brown hair and a calm friendly demeanour.

Having introduced myself and showing him my Police Staff ID card, we shook hands and I ran through the process of taking a swab. I explained that two swabs would be taken, one from each cheek, they would be sealed and submitted to the forensic science laboratory for testing. His DNA profile would be tested only against the Melanie Road murder crime scene DNA profile and would then be destroyed.

Christopher signed two consent forms which I ran through with him and both forms contained the details of the offence under investigation namely the murder of Melanie Road in Bath in June 1984. Christopher showed no sign of nerves, not any more than any of the hundreds of people I had swabbed before. I asked him if he wished to be notified when the results came back, which would be in five to six weeks and he stated that he would like a call on his mobile phone. After the samples had been taken and sealed away, we shook hands and said our goodbyes.

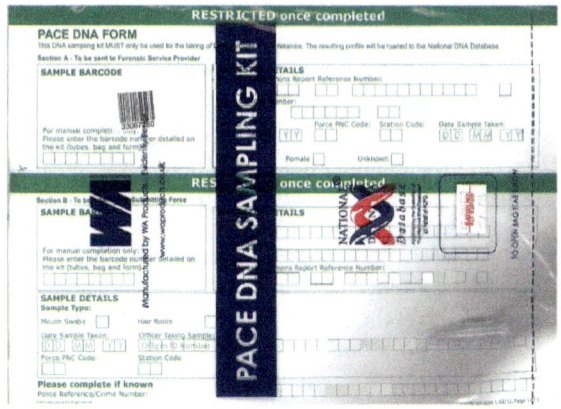

DNA sampling kit

2015 image of
Christopher
Hampton

I drove on to Swansea in Wales and went through the same procedure with Gerry Jones at midday. On returning to the police station, I placed the samples in a secure freezer and submitted all the paperwork into the incident room. Incident room sounds quite glamorous, but it consisted of me and an Indexer Val Farley.

All swabs were submitted in bunches of 30 – 50 to Cellmark where they were processed by Mike Wheelhouse. Whilst this was going on, I was carrying out further searches and doing further swabbing. Christopher Hampton had reached the status of 'Target of the month' but we had been there before and knew only too well not to get excited.

In the whole time of requesting voluntary swabs from people, there were only nine men that refused. They had their reasons, normally their mistrust of the police or the justice system or the fact that they believed it breached their human rights. For most of these nine people, they were still forensically eliminated by approaching other suitable members of their family. There is always more than one way to reach your goal. A total of 2,552 males were eliminated up until this stage.

Just after 9:00am on Thursday 2nd July, I was sat at my desk in Kenneth Steele House, St Phillips, Bristol, where the MCIU were based, once again alone in the incident room. I had a swab planned for 2:30pm that afternoon but it was locally in Bristol. I heard the 'ping', announcing a new e-mail had arrived and I clicked to open it up.

My heart started to beat faster; I couldn't believe what I was reading. Mike was claiming to have a DNA match for the Melanie Road murder and was going to double and triple check it first. Mike stated in his e-mail that he would be out the office for a couple hours. Having only just received the message, I hoped that I might catch Mike before he went off to his meeting. Mike's phone was answered almost immediately but it was a female voice who politely told me that Mike had left. It was one of the longest 2 hour waits of my career. I decided to cancel my 2:30 appointment and to have a look at the recent batch of swab submissions I had sent to Mike in a hope of working out who it was.

Hi,

I think I finally have good news regarding operation Rhodium

I'm currently double and triple checking everything and have also requested the original files, so this is all to be confirmed. However, I'M pretty confident we have a DNA match to one of the last elimination samples sent in.

I've got to go to a case conference on another job this morning but should only be a couple of hours. Can you give me a call please or drop me an email with best contact number and we can hopefully chat later

Mike Wheelhouse's text to me regarding DNA match

Could it be Gerry Jones' brother? He had murdered someone or so the rumour claimed but I knew all about false rumours from the David Baker swab. Could it be Christopher Hampton? He had been too calm to be a guilty person giving a swab knowing it would prove he was a murderer. Could it be one of the two swabs that other people had taken? 30 names were on the list and none of them stood out as the obvious offender.

Mike was finding it difficult to concentrate at the case conference, he was sure in his own mind that the DNA match in the Melanie Road case was solid and no matter how many further checks were made, it would prove to be correct. He planned to phone me as soon as he got back into the office and didn't realise how desperate I was with the delay.

Finally, Mike made the phone call and supplied me with the name of Christopher Hampton for the DNA match. It had already been double checked since his email message so there was no doubt. I asked Mike how good a match it was and he explained that the statistics showed that the chances of it being someone else were 1 billion to 1. This was the highest figure that forensic scientists ever quoted. We could now put a name to the attacker.

There was no-one else working on the investigation yet again and Julie was on a well-deserved holiday out of the country but due back that day. I tracked down the head of the MCIU, Liz Tunks, who had limited knowledge of the case and her first reaction was "*Tell no-one*". Christopher Hampton would be expecting to hear about the result in about one week's time and it was essential that we sought his arrest as soon as possible in case he decided to leave the country or worse, kill himself. Liz tried to phone and text Julie to let her know what was happening and I started enquiries to plan for Hampton's arrest. Hampton would be arriving home in Fishponds at 4:30pm after finishing work and an arrest team needed to be there to detain him immediately.

Liz called for a short supervisory briefing, which I also attended. We needed to discuss search teams, arrest teams and interview teams that would be required to work overtime after Hampton's arrest. It was decided that I was to be used in the incident room as I was the only one who knew the case intimately and could brief up others. Julie should have been back in the country by now, but Liz had heard nothing. I tried Julie's personal mobile number and she picked up straight away. *"We've just had a DNA hit and it's the father of that girl on the familial list"* I explained. *"Bloody hell, we've done it"* was the only response Julie could come up with. *"I'm on my way in."*

Julie arrived 25 minutes later and walked straight across the incident room and gave me a big hug. *"I knew it would happen and I'm so pleased it was you who swabbed the person. It had to be you, that's justice."* Other than a quick chat with Liz, Julie's first priority was to go and tell Melanie's mother and family. They had to hear the news from us and not the media.

Christopher was arrested from home, and he said nothing on arrest, but as he was taken from the house in custody, his wife said: *"I'll see you later"* to which Christopher responded: *"No you won't"*, he even responded the same when his wife said she would see him the following day. He knew he would never be a free man from that day on.

A search team spent 4 hours searching the house for any possible evidence including any historic images of Christopher Hampton from around 1984. In the garage, Christopher kept all the tools of his trade and on display on the garage wall was an old odd-looking knife.

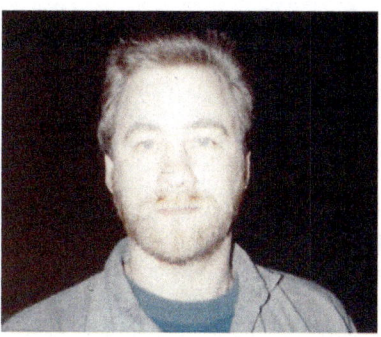

1984 image of Christopher Hampton

Knife found in Hampton's garage

Surely, he would not have kept the murder weapon. This knife would need to be submitted to Mike Wheelhouse and his team of scientists to examine.

The forensic work was about to start a new phase and the latest DNA 17 technology would be used which looks at 16 sites (32 alleles) and even more accurate than earlier techniques.

The contact with the Road family had been maintained over the years. Every time the case was reviewed or any new media publicity was planned, the family would be informed. Anthony Road had possibly suffered the greatest, as he had been placed in a residential care home due to dementia and he had little understanding of what was happening. Jean Road answered the door to Julie, she still lived in the house Melanie had lived in. Julie and Jean had become good friends over the years and Julie told her about having identified Melanie's killer. Jean sometime later said to Julie, "*I knew you would, you always told me you would, I just hoped I would still be alive when you did.*" They shared a cup of tea together as Julie explained the long court process that would follow. Adrian Road, Melanie's brother had got fed up and frustrated with all the updates over the years and the fact that the case appeared to be getting nowhere, he had told the police previously that he did not wish to see them again unless it was to be told that the killer had been caught. Julie delivered that message to him and he broke down in tears saying "*Thank you.*" Karen, Melanie's sister was very matter of fact, the whole experience had had a terrible effect on her and she had almost locked herself away from contact with her family.

Christopher Hampton was interviewed and as is common practice, he produced a prepared statement which read '*I did not rape or murder Melanie Road*'. He answered no comment to all other questions put to him. Even now he was not going to come clean and relieve the intense pressure on Melanie's family. Julie had a long, heated discussion with the Crown Prosecution Service and they eventually agreed that Hampton should be charged with rape and murder. He remained totally impassive when he was charged and returned to his cell to await court the following morning.

It was all change in the incident room, people were suddenly interested and wanted to be involved in this fascinating case. There were suddenly two sergeants permanently engaged on the enquiry and about 20 members of staff. Enquiry officers were sent out to speak with all of Christopher's associates to get some background history about his life from 1984 to present day. Intelligence researchers were used to identify vehicles he had owned over the years, addresses he had and any criminal history. It was surprising how little was discovered about him.

In June 1984, he had been linked to two addresses, both were within ½ a mile of the murder scene. One address was in Broad Street, Bath which was on the route Melanie was known to have walked home that fateful evening, the second address was Great Bedford

Street in Bath which he shared with his girlfriend Dawn. Dawn had been pregnant back in 1984 and her medical records confirmed that she had a termination in August of that year.

Hampton's family described him as a quiet man who would go off to work each day and when he returned home would eat and sit quietly in front of the TV. There were very few examples of any violence or aggression. He once punched his ex-partner in the face for no apparent reason, knocking her unconscious. A work colleague recalled an incident when they were painting in a girl's school and Hampton was disturbed in a storeroom reading from a soft porn magazine. None of this was of great enough significance to be use in court.

The police spoke with Christopher's ex-wife and mother of Clare and Rachael. She had very little information that could assist. Clare was feeling very guilty that she was the reason that her father was now in custody. She could not accept that her father could be the evil man who had raped and murdered an innocent 17-year-old. She provided a statement about how on 28th May 2015, her father had phoned her in a furious temper for the fact that he was now being asked to supply his DNA due to her stupid behaviour with her boyfriend. She thought his reaction was a little excessive but looking back I suppose it is understandable.

Hampton's current wife Julie and her daughter Alice were spoken to. They were convinced that he was innocent and it was all a terrible forensic mistake. They were to stand by him right up until the court case.

The whole case would now need to be entered onto the HOLMES system in some form because it needed to be managed and searchable. The details of males named in the investigation only were on the computer but that soon changed. All the material gathered over the past 30 years would need to be disclosed to the defence. Having an excellent working knowledge of HOLMES and knowing the case, I was able to advise on how best we could achieve getting the material entered onto the computer. All the gathered documentation was brought into the incident room and placed in cabinets to await entering on HOLMES and each item required assessing by disclosure officers. On a normal murder investigation, one disclosure officer is given the task of disclosure, but the magnitude of operation Rhodium meant a sergeant and 7 officers were used.

My main task was to liaise closely with Cellmark and the Forensic Science Service archive staff to build on the forensic evidence. I was also tasked to ensure any exhibit continuity issues were addressed. I was keen to locate the soft porn magazines that should have been amongst the police exhibits as this had been found near to the garages in Camden Row. I wanted to submit this item to the fingerprint department who could use new techniques to find fingerprints. If Hampton's prints could be found, it would possibly give an indication where he first approached Melanie. The magazines were nowhere to be found.

Was there anything else besides the magazines that could be considered for fingerprint analysis. Not only had the fingerprint testing improved over the years but there was the National Automated Fingerprint Identification System (N.A.F.I.S). This was the system I had used in the Kath Thomas rape enquiry.

Files on display in the incident room

Me checking the old card index system

It was known from the forensic evidence dating back to 1984 that one of Melanie's shoes had, at some point, been removed from her foot and later replaced. I checked the investigation paperwork, and it was clear that they had been preserved for fingerprinting and returned from the laboratory at one stage specifically for fingerprinting. What was not within the file was any results. It wouldn't be a problem re-submitting them. Julie agreed and soon both shoes were at the police fingerprinting department being treated with chemicals in a hope they would reveal new evidence. A reasonable finger impression was lifted from the underside of Melanie's right shoe; it was located in the centre of the sole by the arch of the foot. This was considered to be very significant as the location was not where a wearer would normally hold a shoe so could be the attacker's print. The print was loaded onto NAFIS and left for an overnight search. The frustration was back, as it was reported the following morning that no match had been found. This was not Hampton's print either.

It now had to be established whether the fingerprint could have come from any other explained source so a timeline for the shoe since it came into the possession of the police was created. Anyone who had ever touched the shoe would need to be traced and their fingerprints taken for comparison. The 30-person long list mainly consisted of current and retired police and forensic personnel. One at a time they were located and their prints submitted. It was number 19 on the list that eventually answered the question. She was a forensic assistant that had worked at the FSS and been involved in the examination of the shoes after they had been returned from fingerprinting at police HQ. The impression was of her index finger. On the one hand I was disappointed that I did not have Hampton's fingerprint but at least it was accounted for and nothing for the defence to use.

The FSS archives had stated that all forensic material in the Melanie Road murder investigation had already been supplied to Cellmark and that no further evidence was held by them. As a good review officer, I never believed what I was being told and I submitted a further 40 separate requests to the archive storage facility seeking sub-exhibits such as material cut from the victim's trousers in earlier testing in 1984, forensic slides and tapings, DNA extract material. I was aware, for example, that when each of the blood spots had been swabbed, the swab and tip had been placed in tubes. Some of the swab material was then used to test at the laboratory and DNA material extracted. Each of these processes produced sub-exhibits and some remains of the original swab or container they were kept in. I had known cases where apparently empty storage tubes had been found to contain DNA from material previously stored in the tube, so each sub-item was a possible source of material for future testing. Having been originally told there was no material left, a total of 155 items were found and later supplied to Cellmark.

One example was the victim's own blood samples that I had been told were no longer with the lab. This had resulted in the scientists having to work out what the victim's DNA profile had to be from other family members profiles (known as a surrogate profile). I now came into possession of 5 separate samples of the victim's blood, ranging from emptied phials, test spots on blotting paper and slides. It was from these that Mike was able to obtain a full DNA 17 profile of Melanie Road. The SGM+ part of this profile matched the surrogate profile that the scientists had calculated from Melanie's bra, knickers and family members. It would be much more straightforward having a confirmed DNA profile rather than surrogate profile.

Christopher Hampton had a further evidential DNA swab taken from him after arrest as well as blood samples taken. The swab produced a full DNA 17 profile that matched the voluntary swab I had taken in June.

The blood trail had consisted of 80+ blood spots and the evidence to date had identified some as Christopher Hampton's on SGM+ DNA and others as Hampton's blood on blood group A   2-1+. Although the forensic strategy was to test these spots again with DNA 17 techniques, it was clear that they would not all deliver results. The more spots that could be attributable to Hampton the better as they would indicate to the jury the severity of the injury he had sustained and negate any suggestion of a consensual sexual act. It was therefore decided to test Hampton's blood by the old PGM method and to prove that he had blood group A   2-1+. This proved harder than expected as none of the equipment for this type of testing was now available and the only person identified who may be able to assist was Dr Syndercombe-Court based at Kings College London. She used a molecular system that was able to accurately obtain PGM blood results. Surprisingly, this more modern method was not as good as the historic methods and Dr Syndercombe-Court was only able to state that Hampton's blood group was group A 2-1+ or group A 2+1-. It did not contradict the evidence but was not as positive as we had hoped.

The knife recovered from Hampton's garage was then the target of Mike's attention. It was taken apart and tested for blood. The results were disappointing, no blood was found meaning that it was either not the murder weapon or had been very thoroughly cleaned. The knife was shown to a pathologist along with the post-mortem photographs and he concluded that it was not the murder weapon as the blade was not consistent with the injuries.

The victim's intimate samples were the next to be examined and surely these would reveal something additional. The remains of the semen from the oral swab material when tested and produced a full DNA 17 profile which matched the full DNA 17 profile of Christopher Hampton. This was described as a billion to 1 match statistic. Mike was not satisfied with that alone and he went on and tested the oral swab further and obtained the victim's DNA from this swab as well proving it was an oral swab taken from her. This not only proved that the samples tested were from Melanie's oral swab but also the semen was Christopher Hampton's. There were discussions between Mike and I about the possibility of testing the victim's stomach contents for semen, I wanted to know whether a positive result would be able to confirm that the victim was alive at the time of oral sex. Not enough research had been done to prove that spermatozoa could not have travelled into the stomach even in a deceased person so this line of testing was not to be pursued.

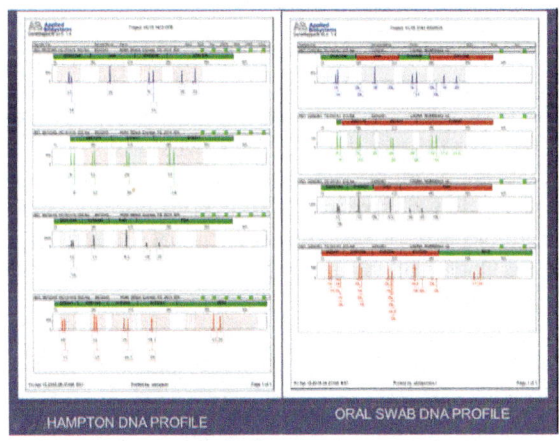

HAMPTON DNA PROFILE   ORAL SWAB DNA PROFILE

DNA comparison chart

The high vaginal swab again tested negative for DNA and would take the case nowhere. The only evidence this swab had ever given was very early positive tests for semen.

The external vaginal swabs produced a partial DNA 17 profile which could also be reported as a billion to 1 match to Hampton.

The victim's trousers had been submitted to the lab several times over the years for testing but had been stored with the police at the Bourneville archive storage unit and they were sent out again to Cellmark. I had located numerous sub- exhibits at the FSS archives and these included small pieces of material cut from semen staining on the trousers for testing. Mike set about his DNA 17 testing and the cut pieces of material taken from semen stains on the trousers produced a full DNA17 profile which matched Hampton's DNA. Mike then used his childhood skills of completing jigsaw puzzles and was able to prove that the pieces of material came from the trousers. The waist band of the trousers produced a full DNA 17 profile of Melanie Road confirming they were her trousers. He could further prove the pieces of the material were from her trousers and the semen on the pieces of material were Hampton's.

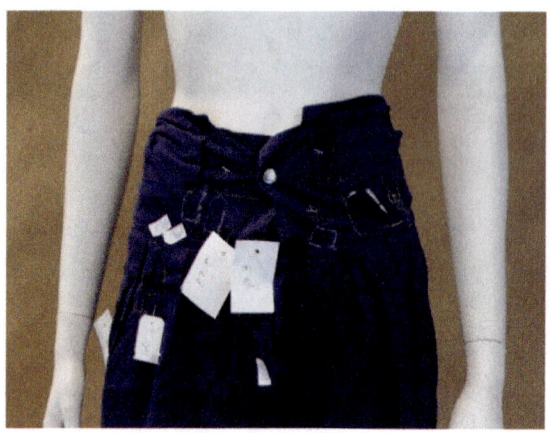

Melanie's trousers

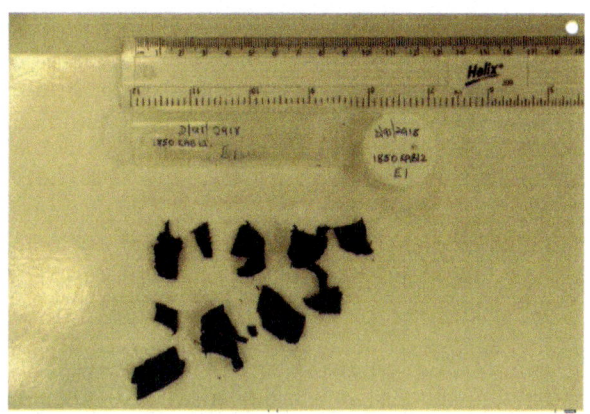

Fragments of material cut from semen stains on Melanie's trousers in 1984

Melanie's knickers were then examined and the pattern of the blood staining on the rear was quite distinctive and matched the pattern on Melanie's trousers. This was compelling evidence that the knickers had been removed some time after Melanie had sustained her injuries and had bled out onto her clothes. The knickers had been removed with Melanie already badly injured or deceased. The sexual act had then taken place before the trousers were replaced. It was afterwards that the knickers had been relocated a short distance away, probably taken by the offender. A minute trace of semen with two possible sperm was found on the front centre panel of the knickers but nothing in the gusset. The semen yet again provided a billion to 1 match to Hampton. This finding suggested to Mike Wheelhouse that the semen on the victim's knickers was unlikely due to them being worn after the sexual assault but more likely transferred onto the knickers from them coming into contact with semen on another item such as someone's hand.

The bra, blouse and cardigan had none of Christopher Hampton's DNA found on them. They did however provide some evidence in relation to cuts and stab wounds on the body.

Mike Wheelhouse had worked so hard and the results were excellent. Mike decided after consultation that DNA 17 testing on the blood spots would be limited to selected spots. Partial DNA 17 profiles from spots 47 and 52 gave billion to 1 match to Christopher Hampton. Blood spots 20, 43 and 45 provided billion to 1 match to Melanie Road. The blood trail had given up its evidence and showed the trail of Melanie's blood dripping into St Stephen's Court as she was carried there and the blood spots in St Stephen's Road and down the steps were from Christopher Hampton leaving the crime scene.

Blood spot chart

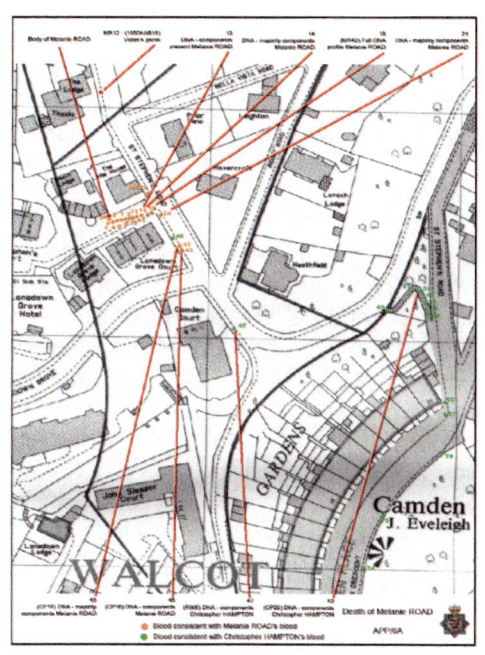

Julie and I, along with other key members of the investigation team, attended several case conferences to decide on how to present the evidence which evidence to use and which to leave on file. Ben Schwarzkopf was the subject of a lot of discussion. He could provide evidence of the victim with a male close to the deposition site. He had already identified the female that he saw as being Melanie. A video identification procedure was carried out to see if he was able to identify Hampton from the

1984 image the police had of him but the passage of 30 years was going to make it highly unlikely. Schwarzkopf hesitated between identifying Hampton and another image but was unable to make a clear identification. Could the defence argue that Schwarzkopf had not identified Hampton because it was not him who was talking to Melanie. Decision made, the case was very strong and introducing Schwarzkopf could cloud the waters.

Should any evidence be introduced regarding the occasional aggression displayed by Hampton and his activity in the girl's school. The defence may suggest that the prosecution was desperate by feeling the need to blacken his name because they were not confident in their case. Decision was made to leave that evidence out.

The barrister, Kate Brunner QC was also keen to withdraw the charge of rape and leave Hampton facing only a murder charge. The discussions surrounded whether an offence of rape could be proven. It was reasonable to argue that the sexual act must have been non-consensual due to the injuries to both the victim and Hampton but could it be proven that the sexual act of vaginal penetration took place and, if it did take place, was it before death. A recent case had been argued in court that a suspect had come across a dead body in the street and had committed a sexual act with the dead body (necrophilia) but he had not been the murderer and it had not been rape because the victim was deceased. Could this be what Hampton was going to say? To avoid the jury listening to hours of defence arguments regarding the offence of rape it was agreed to withdraw that charge and simplify any trial to be one of guilty or not guilty of murder.

The process of disclosure had to be dealt with and this had to be done in accordance with the 1984 disclosure rules and not as current procedures required. This was going to mean that every single document would have to be listed and assessed. Schedules supplied to the defence and giving them copies of any material they wished. There were in excess of 30,000 documents so it was all hands to the pump. The old disclosure system did not require the defence to inform the prosecution what evidence they were disputing so there would be no further information about what Hampton claimed had occurred that night.

Each day new forensic results were being reported and the defence were being hit with powerful evidence of their client's guilt. There were rumours (the team had learnt how reliable rumours could be) that Hampton was going to plead guilty to murder.

The trial was due to start on 9th May 2016 and the Road family was sat in the public gallery within the court. I was with Julie and about 6 members of the investigation team sat just behind the family. The journalists filled the press seats and were allowed to occupy the jury seats because there were so many of them and no jury was required at this stage of the proceedings. Christopher Hampton was asked to stand up and the charge was read out to him.

"*How do you plead*?" There was a one-word answer "*Guilty.*" An immediate buzz filled the court. There were tears from Jean Road, Adrian and Karen, their wait for justice had come to an end. Julie and I both fought back the tears and had to stop ourselves from shouting out in joy "*YES*". The Journalists started writing rapidly into their notebooks. I looked around to my left and behind me and could see the prison guard with tears in her eyes but stood emotionless besides her was Christopher Hampton with an ice-cold blank expression on his face. This was the man who at last admitted brutally murdering Melanie and had lived the last 32 years as if he had done nothing wrong.

Before he was to sentence Christopher Hampton, the judge asked to hear statements from the Road family about how the murder of Melanie had impacted on their life. Jean, Adrian and Karen in turn got up and entered the witness box to read out their impact statements. They all had different things to say and for the first time they understood how each other had suffered in their own way. The statements were so difficult to listen to but only one person in the court room was not moved by them. It does not seem right to precis what the family had to say so their entire statements are recorded:

Jean Road

My name is Jean Road and I am the mother of Melanie Road. On the 9th June 1984 at 9:15am our world fell apart. As we heard and saw a police car by the window, the officer was calling out Melanie's name. I ran out of the house, caught up with the car, frantically banging on the boot 'stop, please stop'. The police officer escorted me back to the house and that's when all hell let loose as our lives were taken over by the tragedy and horror when hearing of our daughter's death. As we waded through the questions, identification and all that proceeds after a death as Melanie's, the impact it had on our individual lives was and still is devastating. We forgot to eat, sleep was interrupted with constant nightmares. We lost weight. I wondered aimlessly through the streets of Bath hoping to see a glimpse of Melanie. Searching the places, we had visited together.

Where Melanie's blood was spilled, I prayed that it would not rain to wash it away, and when it did, I cursed the rain for finally taking it away. I felt even the weather was against Melanie and the family. We sat for hours traumatised by the horror of knowing Melanie was gone forever. To never see her beautiful smile and girlish laughter hurts beyond repair. We were not functioning properly. We constantly had no energy. My husband refused to talk to me about Melanie. I never knew if he discussed his feelings with anyone else in the family or at work. Therefore, it was inevitable that we drifted apart. But we kept an artificial pretence to outsiders. Little did they know how we were suffering?

Our son Adrian (Melanie's brother) was at the Nautical College in Glasgow. Our daughter Karen was in Solihull with her husband and two young children. They were notified by the police. When I spoke to Adrian, he said, 'I can't cope I'm coming home'. This meant that he missed taking his final exams. We felt his future was now ruined.

Karen arrived in Bath with her baby who was 7 weeks old. She was breastfeeding her child but the shock upon hearing of Melanie's death caused her milk to dry up. Luckily, at 11:30pm the female WPC and RUH came to Karen's rescue and provided formula and a supply of feeding bottles until Karen could rest.

The huge impact of the horror of Melanie's death permeated throughout the family members, grandparents, aunts, uncles, all relations including school friends. Who knows what harm it has done to them? My husband returned to work, not sure if he was functioning properly there because he certainly was not functioning when at home. It was suggested I go back to work teaching, but I could not have borne the responsibilities of other people's children after what had happened to Melanie. We put on a face for the outside world. Once asleep, I hoped I would never wake up so that I could be with Melanie and comfort her.

I couldn't and wouldn't speak to the few people I had got to know in Bath, (we had only been here 2 years) because for fear that they would tell me how to cope! I mistrusted everyone! I wanted to gather my other children and family together and disappear forever!! Yes, people were kind in sending letters, cards and flowers for which I was thankful but I wanted Melanie not these gifts, but that was not going to happen.

The thought of what our lovely daughter had to endure on that fateful night still sucks the energy from within me. The horror of the way our daughter died hangs over us like a heavy lead weight which never moves away. Some days, I think I have moved on with my life but energy forsakes me and the weight presses further and further down. Sadly, Melanie's father, my husband, now lives in a haze of Dementia hastened by our daughter's death. When will this pain stop? The horror of that sunny day in June will never leave us!

Our patience has been tested but we have survived these 31 ½ years not without heartache and sorrow, whilst we have waited for justice to take its course to hopefully allow Melanie to R.I.P. I was 49 years old in 1984 when all this happened. Now in my 81st year, I pray that the family will find some peace. Over the past 30 years we have gradually been torn apart by this evil deed. Nothing will bring Melanie back, but I pray that the rest of the family can again be reunited.

Karen Road

I am the sister of Melanie Road. You would think nothing could be worse than being told your little sister had been sexually assaulted and murdered in the most brutal way. But it can get worse – no one was charged for my sister Melanie's murder for 31 years. People often tell me what a beautiful or safe place Bath is. When they tell me this, I just keep quiet. I think about my sister Melanie. I'd always longed for a baby sister, and when she was born in 1966, I thought all my prayers had been answered. She was pretty, sweet and clever. We used to call her a 'little duckling' – with her NHS glasses, with a patch over one eye. I knew she was going to turn into a beautiful swan one day, and she did.

The last time I saw Melanie was at 5pm outside the Francis Hotel in Queen's Square, Bath. I remember it perfectly – she leant over and kissed me on the cheek to say goodbye. We'd spent that week together. She was only 17 – beautiful, popular, and bright. She was going off to play tennis with her friends. She was about to do her A Levels, and she was looking forward to going out with friends that evening. She had her whole life ahead of her, the whole world was opening up for her.

Later that night, Melanie was brutally murdered as she walked home. On June 9th, 32 years ago, I learned the horrific truth – that Melanie had been murdered. For me and my family, nothing has ever felt safe again. I don't believe in 'safe' any more. I've replayed that last kiss, that last evening, countless times in my mind: 'If I had stayed with her, if I had only gone with her that night ... if only I could have saved her'. It's a particular kind of torture that accompanies murder that settles in the mind.

At the time, we were told that Melanie had been stabbed 26 times, that she had suffered some kind of sexual assault, that she had been attacked, and left – as it turned out – heartbreakingly close to her home. In the absence of any more information, my imagination filled in the gaps. I've had 32 years to fill in the gaps. Melanie has died hundreds of times, in hundreds of different ways in my mind – while I'm awake, while I'm asleep. I could tell you that it's like being in a nightmare, but you wake from a nightmare, and life returns to normal. This is a nightmare I can't ever wake up from.

I haven't wanted my whole life to be defined by murder. But it has been. Melanie's death has consumed my life, and it's been frightening. For 32 years I've felt as if I'm living in a horror film – one where the perpetrator has not been caught. Not knowing who is responsible for Melanie's death has been torture. I can't explain the impact of not knowing who the murderer is, where he is. Is he nearby? Is it someone we know? Does he know who we are? Or wondering who's next? My body and mind have been on red alert since 9th June 1984. It's exhausting. It's affected every aspect of my life – physically, emotionally, financially, relationships, work, my family, my girls, this nightmare has been their life – there's not a single thing that has not suffered as a consequence of Melanie's death, and my suffering has been magnified by the horrific nature of her death.

Grief is a lonely place. Grief caused by murder is lonelier. Having a sister is a special bond. Losing the sister, I had longed for – and in such a violent, callous way – has left me traumatised. For years I was unable to retrieve any happy memories of Melanie, and was constantly reliving her death. Her death has been all-encompassing and has defined her life as well as mine. I want to be able to remember her life, rather than the focus being forever on her horrific last hours. Melanie has disappeared. Since her death she's been a statistic, a crime to be solved, a court case. But she's my sister. She's a person, she deserves to be remembered for herself – caring, kind, sensible, and intelligent; she was applying for university. She had dreams and wishes – about being married, having children – we'd talked about that during our last week together. She was due to go to the Greek Islands on holiday. She was excited about life, about going travelling, about her little nieces – that last morning she'd bathed and dressed her youngest niece, a baby of just 6 weeks at the time. And that's the point at which her life, her future, was brutally taken away. If you want to know what it's like to lose a sister in this way, it's impossible to tell you. There's not a cell in my body unaffected. Not a single day passes without me thinking about her. For me, after Melanie's death, everything has been frozen in time, or buried.

Since 9th June 1984, I've hoped, desperately, for her killer to be brought to justice. For 31 years no one was charged for Melanie's murder. It's called a 'cold case'. To me it has never been cold – it occupies all my thoughts, and the police have continued to investigate leads and to re-examine evidence using new technologies.

The impact on me of Melanie's murder not being solved is huge. I have wanted to do anything I can to help find and identify the person who killed my sister. But this inevitably has come at a cost – the physical and emotional effort of trying to maintain a normal life, while waiting for my sister's killer to be found is immeasurable.

I have always wanted to see the good in people. I was brought up to believe people have a conscience, that they own up to the things they do wrong. It has been unimaginable to me that someone could willfully cause such horrific suffering to another human being – to my sister.

There is no 'getting over' such a loss, such a death. I've longed for someone to be caught, but even the news of someone being charged has been very difficult – I've been catapulted emotionally back in time to Day 1 of Melanie's death and I am reliving it all again. I'm glad I didn't know at the time of Melanie's death it would take 31 years for someone to be charged. It's hard to believe that, for 32 years, this evil person has not owned up to his horrific crime, has been willing to let us go on suffering the consequences of his terrible actions.

All I have ever wanted is justice for Melanie. My wish is that Hampton spends the rest of his life in prison and that I will be able to remember my happy memories of Melanie, and for her memory not to be defined by her horrific last hour.

Adrian Road

I am the brother of Melanie Road. Saturday June 9th 1984, a day that I had already planned out as I had my final Navy exams on the Monday, a day that Melanie had planned out as she had final A level exams on the Monday. We had both spoken that week about our exams and how we were going to get really good marks. Her last comments to me as I called her from the Nautical College in Glasgow was best of luck in your exams, I love you. Saturday June 9th 1984, my uncomplicated world as a 22-year-old student collides catastrophically with yours. Melanie didn't get to sit her exams on Monday and neither did I. Because you murdered Melanie. You snuffed out her life and altered my life forever.

I have spent the last 32 years worrying about every man that ever walked down the street, asking myself, "did you kill my little sister Melanie?". Every man that sat near to me in a restaurant, "did you kill my little sister Melanie?". Every man that I have ever met, "could you have killed my little sister Melanie?". Even my friends, "did they kill my little sister Melanie?" But now I know, thankfully, none of them killed Melanie. You did, you killed Melanie, you mutilated her, and you chose to abandon her, you abandoned her when she was dying, my little sister Melanie. You took away a very special person who was so close to me you wouldn't be able to understand or comprehend what she meant to me. She was a lovely girl and I loved her. We all loved her. You couldn't possibly understand how it feels to love another human. You couldn't possibly understand how it feels to show compassion to another person as you chose to murder a defenceless child. A child, only 17. You have no compassion, you have no right, you killed a child. A child who posed no threat to you, a child who was more interested in whether she would get three A levels which would enable her the choice of university, you have no right.

Thirty-two years I have patiently waited for the telephone call to say "Adrian, we have him". Thirty-two years I have listened to dozens of Police Officers assure me "Adrian, we will find him". They were right, they did find you and when they told me, I cried, uncontrollably, I cried. My six-year-old daughter asked me *"Daddy, why are you crying?"* I had to tell her *"The man who killed aunty Melanie, my little sister a long time ago, has now been caught, so we are now safe."* She didn't quite understand, but her innocent face looked up at me and started to think it over and even at her young age her moral compass points in the right direction. Her words to me were *"That is so sad, he needs to be punished."*

Your capture will not bring me closure, it never will, but I can now feel safer that you will be locked away for a very long time. I take little comfort from the ironic thought of you killing someone else's daughter, yet you are paradoxically caught by your own daughter's DNA. As you start your new life of being a convicted child murderer, I will now start my new life of freedom. Freedom from the 32 years of not knowing.

Thank you, my Lord, for letting me express a small but detailed portion of the last 32 years.

The Judge Mr Justice Popperwell

Having heard from the family the Judge made three very moving comments:

"The statements read out with great dignity by her mother, sister and brother, testify that every day for the last 32 years, they have been suffering the agony of losing Melanie in such horrific circumstances."

"You lived your family life for all those years knowing the extreme misery you must have inflicted on your victim's family but were too callous and cowardly to put an end to it."

"I have to determine how long it will be before you are eligible for release. That does not mean that you will be released at the end of your minimum term I set. You will likely die in prison."

Hampton was then sentenced to life imprisonment with a minimum term of 22 years before parole could be considered. He was taken down from the dock to the cells below to start his sentence. The Judge commended a number of officers for the meticulous and tenacious investigation, specifically naming Julie and me.

As they left the court room, Jean gave Karen a massive hug. This was the first loving physical contact they had shown to each other for more than 30 years. Everyone grieves in different ways, some like to talk about their grief and others like to shut it away. The differing grieving needs within the Road family had broken them apart and the signs were there that the mending process was starting.

The cold-case guru on killers' trail

The media interest

A large group of reporters was waiting outside Bristol Crown Court for interviews with Julie and I. Jean for the first time, gave an interview that was shared between all the media and the story hit the headlines. Was the success of this investigation down to luck? Well, you make your own luck and I believe the success was down to the attitude of those involved, you can make your own mind up. The case would not have reached a successful conclusion had it not been for the various Senior Investigating Officers, Forensic Scientists, Pathologist, Scenes of Crime Officers and Police Officers from 1984 who were so thorough in their investigation and gathering as well as storing of the forensic evidence. Had it not been for the Review Officers and Forensic Scientists over the years then the DNA evidence would never have been discovered. The female police officer who chose to swab Clare Hampton after a relatively minor criminal damage offence was an essential part of the puzzle. You must never forget the scientist who researched and discovered DNA as without him none of this would have been possible and Hampton would still be a free man today. I like to think that had it not been for Julie's and my own dogged determination and refusal to give up, Hampton would never have been identified. So many people had contributed to the success of this case and Julie wanted to thank them all.

In a statement made to the media Jean Road said *"I would like to thank the police and their team for their dedication and perseverance to at last bring this case to a close. Their generosity of time and compassion shown to the Road family has been outstanding. Thank you forever. Now may she rest in peace."* Hearing this comment from Jean meant so much to me personally and the team, it is why we do our job.

A presentation evening was arranged for those involved, where police officer's past and present were invited to attend. Malcolm had died but his widow wanted to come along as she knew how much the case had meant to her husband. Forensic scientists were there and even some of Melanie's family and friends. The atmosphere was a cheerful one but one thing that came up time and time again in conversation was:

- Why did it happen?
- What exactly happened?
- Has Hampton committed any other offences?

None of these questions would ever be answered unless Hampton chooses to speak out. The Review team did look into the possibility that Hampton was responsible for the murder of Shelly Morgan only days after Melanie was murdered. There was no forensic evidence available on that case as her body was badly decomposed when it was discovered. In December 1984 Consultant Psychiatrist Dr David Mawson from Broadmoor provided a profile for the offender. He identified unusual behavioural traits and rage and hatred towards women, probable mental health issues and the likelihood of the offender deteriorating, possibly moving into spree offending until interrupted by arrest or being sectioned. He suggested possible links to the Shelly Morgan murder. She had been repeatedly stabbed. He felt the chances of two people with such extreme mental pathology committing offences so close together (12 miles and two days apart) were, in his experience remote. I quote 'Given the low incidence of sexually motivated homicides, which at least in part we must assume both to have been and given the low incidence of these in the area, it is extremely improbable that two such events would occur so closely together other than as the result of the actions of one man.' There is nothing that can be done until

Hampton decides he wants to admit his offending history and seeing the kind of person he clearly is, I have little expectation that Hampton will speak.

Julie was promoted within 12 months to Detective Chief Inspector in Gloucestershire Constabulary and I moved on to my next case, the murder of Susan Donoghue. Julie and I still met up several times a year at various conferences where we would present operation Rhodium to law students, SIO's and Review Officers.

My efforts were recognised by the national Homicide working group who presented me with the award for my services to homicide investigations and named me as the top police staff member for 2016. Julie and I both attended a presentation ceremony to receive our Crown Court Commendation from Chief Constable Andy Marsh.

Crown Court Commendation award

Jean Road was often visited by Julie, who would always stop for a cuppa and chat. The relationship between Jean and her daughter slowly improved. Jean died aged 87 but at least she did so knowing that her daughter's killer had been brought to justice.

The case was further recognised on the international stage when Julie and I were invited to attend the DNA Hit of the Year Awards in Rome in 2018 where Operation Rhodium was declared the top case of the year, beating murder investigations from China and the USA into third and second places.

Julie and I receiving recognition at the 2018 DNA Hit of the Year Awards

Me speaking at the at the 2018 DNA Hit of the Year Awards in Rome

I have now retired fully but all my awards are proudly on display in my office at home. At the time of my retirement, the hierarchy within the Avon and Somerset police were slowly moving away their support for cold case work and their priorities were moving to other areas of policing. I left at a time when there were still many cold cases that were very detectable. It needs the right staff and right support and just a little luck and the results will continue. I can think of two other familial cases that I hope to see being reported as detected on the local news one day in the near future. These cases have full offender DNA profiles.

The first being the murder of Susan Donaghue in August 1976, who was attacked and sexually assaulted whilst ill in bed in her bedsit at Downleaze, Sneyd Park Bristol. The second being the attack of a young mother who was walking along the A370 at Hewish in 1984, when she was dragged into a ditch and raped. If the offenders are still alive then beware, I hope one day soon, cold case detectives will come knocking on their door.

Preview of other books in the series

If you enjoyed reading 'The Cold Case Detective' then you may also be interested in the other books in the series by the same author Gary Mason. 'The Murder Detective' and 'The Vice Detective'.

The Murder Detective:

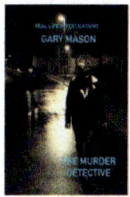

Follows me working on three different murder cases and a manslaughter investigation during my years in the Avon and Somerset Police. They are only a few of the murders that I have worked on, but each was in a different role and are fascinating for different reasons.

The first case is the murder of shopkeeper Roy Page in 1985. Roy was running a sweetshop in St John Lane, Bedminster, Bristol, when a mysterious man, purporting to be a Gas board official, called at his shop and beat him to death. I was called in on day 1 to carry out Exhibit Officer duties for the investigation and also sat through the trial as the investigation reached its conclusion. The case shows the power of the media and the public, who between them identified the offender and directed the police to arrest the man. It details the bizarre account given by the offender in an attempt to avoid conviction.

The second case was in 1998 and I will lead you through the investigation into the murder of Jenny King, a 22-year-old girl, who was attacked and murdered whilst walking home from a night club in Kingswood, Bristol. I was working in the incident room and was the case officer throughout the trial. You will learn about the recovery of a vast amount of evidence and how several experts were able to prove the case against Paul Hunt as well as how evidence nearly pointed towards two innocent men.

The third case is the murder of Patrick Logan in 2000 during a robbery at his home in Castlejordan, Co Meath, Ireland. I will detail how Detective Constable Ian Hieron and I worked closely with the Garda and using our initiative and untried methods recovered important evidence that enabled the Garda to arrest the offenders for the murder and secure convictions.

The manslaughter tells the tragic tale surrounding the accidental death of a university student in 1992. The battles to prove the gross negligence of the people responsible for his death in order for his family to feel that someone was being held to account for the death and to prevent future similar occurrences.

The final two cases in this book look at the specific crime described as domestic homicide. I look at a male and female victim who were ferociously attacked. The similar defences put forward by the suspects and the different outcomes on the cases.

The Vice Detective:

Leads you into the seedy world of prostitution with me investigating and dealing with the problem of kerb crawlers in inner city St Pauls, Bristol. I then investigate a man for running several brothels in Bristol, Weston-Super-Mare and Cheltenham. You will learn how the evidence was gathered to secure a prosecution. You will take a look into three drugs operations to bring down drug dealers who supplied heroin and cannabis in south Bristol. The case of a cannabis growing facility discovered in a remote location in Bristol and how evidence was gathered to identify those involved. Finally on the subject of greed you will learn about how the police being too impatient to identify offenders blew their chances to identify people printing counterfeit currency.

Dedication

I would like to dedicate this story to all the brave and courageous victims. They have dealt with so much during the initial assaults and the re-investigations. It is their determination for justice that kept my motivation and drive for relentlessly pursuing the offenders. I give praise to my fellow colleagues in the police and the forensic scientists who do their jobs to help the victims move forward in their lives, I wish the results could be immediate. I continued to hunt down these evil offenders until my retirement in 2020 and then passed on the work to other investigators.

I would like to thank my niece Camille Leveau for her photographic skills in producing the superb book cover and I wish her well in her future in photography.

I must mention my friend Robert Murphy who is a well-respected journalist who I met many times during my career and who has reported on a number of these cases over the years. It was Robert who encouraged me to write this book and has given me support and guidance throughout.

I would also like to make a mention about the three ladies in my life, Bernie, my wife and my two daughters Blandine and Chloe. There were many occasions during my 43 years police service when I was absent from home due to working overtime or cancelled rest days. I hope by reading this story they will understand the reasons for my absences. I would never have had the energy and fighting spirit if they had not been so supportive. I also hope that my grandsons Luca, Marco, Renzo, Jacob and Oscar get a chance to read the story when they are older. I would love them to understand the work that their Papu did in the police.

Gary Mason

About the author

I joined the Avon and Somerset police in March 1977 and was posted as a uniform constable to 'B' Division working predominantly on the Knowle West council estate. I was a prolific thief taker and this resulted in me being successful in my application to become a detective constable based at Bishopsworth Police station in 1983. Between 1983 and 1989 I learnt my trade in crime investigation and was involved in several high-profile investigations. In 1985 I got my first taste of murder investigations when I was the exhibits officer in the investigation into the murder of shop owner Royston Page in Bedminster, Bristol. The case was detected with the help of the media (Crimewatch UK) when an appeal was put out to identify a bogus gas official seen in the area at the time of the murder. I carried out duties in the role of an acting sergeant on the CID until my eventual promotion in 1989. For one-year, I again performed uniform duties as a sergeant covering the St Pauls area of Bristol. Drugs and prostitution were the main social problems that the police were required to deal with. The draw of crime investigation was too much and I jumped at the opportunity to return to CID work in 1990 and was posted to Yeovil CID office. The daily travel from Bristol to Yeovil for a whole year proved too much and I was not seeing enough of my family, my wife Bernie and daughters Blandine and Chloe. I requested to return to Bristol. Between 1991 and 2002, I worked at various CID offices around Bristol, Redland, Southmead, St George and Staplehill and took any opportunity to be seconded to murder investigations where I felt I got the greatest satisfaction. I trained as a scene liaison officer attending murder crime scenes and post-mortems and I became well known for working in major incident rooms using the HOLMES computerised recording system. In October 1998, I was the receiver and case supervisor in one of the Avon and Somerset's largest and most well-known murder investigation, the murder of 22-year-old Jenny King as she walked home from a night club in Kingswood, Bristol. This investigation stirred up a media frenzy which continued until the eventual conviction of Paul Hunt in March 2000. In 2002 the Avon and Somerset police set up a dedicated Major Crime Investigation Unit to investigate all murders in the force area and I was one of 4 detective sergeants selected to be part of this unit. In 2003 the Major Crime Investigation Unit were tasked with setting up a cold case investigation section and I took the lead role in forming a small group of officers and staff to investigate cold case stranger rape offences. I remained working on the MCIU until my retirement after 31 years service in February 2008. With only 2 weeks off, I commenced employment as a crime investigator with the Avon and Somerset police working in their Major Crime Review Team. The MCRT provide support and guidance to senior investigating officers in undetected murders and stranger rape offences and also took on the responsibility of cold case investigations. At the time of writing, I am no longer employed with the police having retired in 2020 after a total of 43 years service. The book contains only a very small number of complex investigations that I worked on.

Printed in Great Britain
by Amazon